Jobs
&
People

New York
City
1985

Jobs
&
People

New York
City
1985

James W. Hughes
George Sternlieb

Published jointly by

Center for Urban Policy Research

&

Citizens Housing and Planning

Council of New York

The Center for Urban Policy Research
P.O. Box 38
New Brunswick, New Jersey 08903

James Hughes is a professor of urban planning at Livingston College and Research Associate at the Center for Urban Policy Research.

George Sternlieb is director of the Center for Urban Policy Research and a professor of urban and regional planning at Rutgers University.

Cover design by Francis G. Mullen.
Typography by Frank Gradilone
Copyright 1978, Rutgers - The State University
    of New Jersey.
All rights reserved.
Published in the United States of America, by
    the Center for Urban Policy Research,
    New Brunswick, New Jersey 08903.

Library of Congress Catalogue card number:
ISBN 0-88285-055-5

Table of Contents

List of Exhibits

Acknowledgments

We would first like to acknowledge the support of the Ford Foundation in making this study possible; the fellowship grant awarded to Professor Hughes permitted the effort to proceed in an uninterrupted fashion.

Connie O. Michaelson, a demographer with the New Jersey Department of Labor and Industry, was instrumental in the design of the model employed in this study; her contributions are difficult to underestimate.

We would also like to acknowledge the Center for Urban Policy Research staff, Mary Picarella, Joan Frantz, Lydia Lombardi, Anne Hummel, and Frank Gradilone.

Needless to say the errors that remain are the authors own.

James W. Hughes
Center for Urban
Policy Research

Introduction

This volume represents the first half of a study which attempts to place in perspective two major housing programs in New York City. They are the 421 program, which provides tax subsidies for new multifamily rental construction; the second, the J-51 program, involves tax abatement plus additional incentives for the rehabilitation of extant structures, mechanisms of increasing visibility as they relate to loft conversions.

In a city convulsed with the basic realities of social delivery requirements in the face of an endemic fiscal squeeze, the necessity for rigorous evaluation of subsidy programs is evident. This is even more strikingly the case when such programs, as detailed in the second volume of this series, excluding secondary effects, largely benefit more affluent members of the community. Moreover, the emulation of New York's programmatic thrusts by other jurisdictions enhances the requirement that their full implications be adequately specified.

In this context, the primary function of this book is to explore the broad future contours of housing demand in New York City, enabling judgements to be made about the market potential of the target populations of the subsidy mechanisms. Given program support, a clientele

shrinking in absolute numbers implies a potential shift
in occupancy from unsubsidized to subsidized shelter
formats, with all the attendant fiscal ramifications. A
market population growing in size - particularly a segment whose retention is vital to the city's future -
provides a completely different rationale for program
formulation. Consequently, the task of this volume is
the projection of the structure of New York's population
over the next decade, linking demographic evolution to
changes in the city's economic base. By providing insight
into likely household configurations and age sectors of
the future population base, we hope to narrow the areas
of uncertainty which surround the city's housing strategy.

New York City's future housing supply, certainly
over the next decade, will largely be determined by the
level of success in maintaining the extant stock. The
2.8 million housing units which presently provide shelter
for New Yorkers, are in a wide range of configurations
and levels of usage. It is an aging stock with approximately half of the rental units more than fifty years
old. The challenges to its continued viability are substantial. One estimate, for example, suggests that
roughly 20,000 or more units per year are presently being
abandoned. Considering that the average level of conventional housing starts is substantially less than
this, the attrition becomes evident.

*Housing policy therefore, in the city, must start
off with a basic requirement of subduing the substantial
leakage from the system.*

At this writing, approximately 25,000 of New York
City's residential structures are tax delinquent for
more than a year, i.e., subject to foreclosure proceed-
ings. If present trends were extrapolated, the city
would find itself having to manage roughly 10 percent of
its total rental stock by the end of 1979. The logis-
tical difficulties of this possibility are enormous.
New York City's Housing Authority has an enviable re-
putation internationally for its competence. Indeed,
despite folklore to the contrary, its units are a much
desired target for low income housing aspirants. Nonetheless, it may well be questioned whether the agency
can cope with the one-of-a-kind, aged structures to
which the city may well fall heir. And, our projections
indicate an increase rather than an alleviation of the
city's need for additional housing.

New York has long accepted a housing shortage as an
unquestionable constant. From 1950 to 1970, the city's
population in total remained relatively constant. During

the same period new construction of housing units approached 700,000. Yet there was little change in a chronically low vacancy rate. This latter result was a tribute to the very rapid changes occuring in the configurations of the city's households. Yet the post-1970 job and population losses have raised considerable question as to the reliability of past assumptions.

The future size of New York City's population revolves around the scale of its economic base. Using a variety of data and trend analysis, our projections indicate a substantial diminution of recent job losses as well as population decline. Yet absolute losses are anticipated. *Again the process of household size shrinkage indicates that this will not provide an abatement of the need for additional housing in the city. Indeed, we project an increase in the number of households through 1985.*

Increasingly, the population of the city is bifurcated, with a swelling tide of relatively low income, largely minority group households contrasting with the white-elderly on the one hand, and relatively young, frequently unmarried and typically childless, a middle-to-upper income group on the other. There are substantial indications that this latter group is growing quite rapidly in proportion - if it is still relatively small in absolute number.

If New York City is to maintain its economic balance, if it is to provide a local economy of depth and potency, the fostering of this element becomes of enormous importance to the future of the poor.

The poor in New York City will continue to live there - and at least in the short run we see, if anything, an extension in the number of low income households. Thus there will be a continued demand for low cost housing. Given the imbalance between rent paying capacities and the construction/maintenance costs of adequate units of subsidization, the Section 8 program, with all of its administrative headaches and limitations, is the most important single potential input in this arena.

But without in any way limiting the levels of attention which have to be focused in this crucial arena, it must be complemented with a broader sweep of endeavor if the city is to avoid becoming a repository solely for the poor. The experience from 1970 to 1975 has reemphasized the linkage between jobs and residents. If the city is to maintain its job base in a post-industrial era, particularly in the face of the new communications technology, its major asset is the highly skilled, technical, managerial professional set which is emerging. Again, let us repeat,

this is not merely to foster the continuance of New York
as truly as Empire City, but rather in the best interest
of its less fortunate occupants as well. Without them,
the city will become a haven for the pensionaries; the
hapless public clients of the future.

Thus, the strong support for brownstoning and other
forms of housing for the new mobile, high-incomed generation comes most importantly upon the scene. And it does
so most strikingly in terms of the new demographics. As
detailed more fully in the material which follows, the
maturation of the baby boom generation has now progressed
to a point which ensures an enormous increase in the 25-
to-44-years-of-age sectors in the period of our forecast.
The survey work which is detailed in our second volume,
provides an excellent profile of the occupants both of
the 421 units and a most promising subset of present
and potential J-51 beneficiaries - the loft convertees.

In sum, these tend to be relatively youthful heads
of households who have distinctively high incomes and
possess skill levels which specifically fit the growth
pattern of the City's future job base. Their household
configurations largely exempt them from the necessity
of depending on some of the more criticized municipal
service systems - most significantly, the public schools.
A very small proportion of the occupants of either
housing configuration, for example, have children of
school age.

The scale of this group is substantial presently
and as our projections indicate, will grow even more so
in the future. Can New York City provide the packages
of housing which are an essential element in both re-
taining present occupants and securing some share of the
future expansion?

There is nothing new about the evolution of a job
base; nothing novel about the decline of old industries.
While those specifically involved in the process may
find a changing industrial base a most trying experience,
from the viewpoint of the overall economy, the results
may be relatively unimportant. But this is only the
case if there is continued replenishment and innovation;
only when there are new jobs and new skills to replace
older requirements.

The United States as a whole is passing through
this process with manufacturing employment deferring to

the new realities of a service economy. New York City
has not merely weathered, but has successfully tri-
umphed over equivalent vagaries in the past. The new
changes are particularly person dependent. They have
not come upon us suddenly - they have been forecasted
for the city as early as a half century ago.

   *If properly implemented, this time of trouble can
end in one of triumph - of a city with a refurbished
job base which looks to the future rather than deferring to the past.*

   The projections presented here are broadly mutable.
They reflect at best, the fragility both of the techniques used and our own in employing them. Most strikingly however, they are changeable depending upon New
York City's generating a positive and virile consensus
for future growth. Despite the trauma of the last half
dozen years New York still has a practically unique
capacity to shape its future. The question is one of
will.

Overview and Summary of Findings

INTRODUCTION

After a decade (1960 to 1970) of virtual stability in size, New York City's economic and demographic profile was altered suddenly to a degree without parallel in the previous half century. The post-1970 changes were so rapid that the conventional wisdom and expectations borne through the 1960s were found to be of limited utility. The city's linkage to a long term transformation in the nation's social and economic dynamics came into definition. No longer were the events of New York interpreted via a framework of urban-suburban competition; increasingly invoked for explanation were the realities of regional shifts; the rise of nonmetropolitan "exurban" territories, the decline of whole metropolitan areas, the exportation of labor intensive economic activities to lower cost foreign areas, and the burgeoning manufacturing role of lesser developed countries. Yet, even though the frame of reference has broadened, the pattern of aftereffect in New York City may represent only the acceleration of past trendlines. Indeed, despite the outward signs of stability, the city was enmeshed in the throes of change through the decade of the 1960s.

1. Between 1960 and 1970, the city's total population fluctuated in the vicinity of 7.9 million people, while its employment base continually registered about 4.0 million jobs.

2. Internally, however, rapid change was manifest.
The city lost almost one-half million people
through migration, the consequence of the loss
of 900,000 whites and the inflow of 400,000 nonwhites. The magnitude of net natural increase
(births minus deaths) barely counterbalanced the
migration losses. Nonwhites increased their proportional share of the city's population from
14.7 percent in 1960 to 23.4 percent by 1970.
And while the city's population experienced considerable losses among the more mature age
sectors (25 to 64 years of age), the surging baby
boom generation (15 to 24 years of age) served
as the locus of growth.

3. Within the economic sector, the stable total job
count was maintained through processes of substitution. The loss of 200,000 manufacturing jobs
was compensated by increases in white collar
employment -- particularly in information-dependent and communications-intensive activities. The
broader postindustrial transformation effected a
relatively smooth transition in the city's
economic structure.

The alteration of society's course in the post-1970
period did not completely blunt the long term trends.
However, the intersection of national shifts with the city's
historic momentum generated a series of painful adjustments.
No longer was the process of change one of substitution
and compensation -- shrinkage and contraction began to
characterize the New York environment.

1. The city's population declined below the 7.5
million person mark between 1970 and 1975.[1] The
long-term decline since 1957 in the national rate
of fertility had an impact on New York City; net
natural increases were no longer sufficient to
counter the effects of outmigration, increasing
the role and prominence of the latter. The
city's outmigration approached 600,000 people
over this five-year span; the net natural
increase of approximately 200,000 individuals
was insufficient to prevent significant population
decline. We estimate the nonwhite populace as
exceeding 31 percent of the city's total in
1975.

2. As in the previous decade, the losses centered
about the more mature age sectors of the city.
Additionally, the baby bust generation -- the
consequence of fertility rate declines -- began

to reinforce the dynamics of contraction
as it matured into the 5 to 14 years-of-age
category. The aging baby boom cohorts, who
were reflected mainly in the 25 to 34 years
of age sector, persisted as a growth locus.

3. The city's economy over the 1970 to 1975 period
    underwent a process of change similar to that of
    its population - a faltering of the growth ele-
    ments which historically had buffered the impact
    of declining sectors. Within five years, New York
    lost 500,000 jobs, the bulk of which were in manu-
    facturing - an extension of past trendlines.[2] How-
    ever, white collar employment not only failed to
    compensate for these losses, it also contributed
    to the matrix of decline. The benefits of the
    post-industrial service transformation tended to
    bypass the city, accruing mainly to the newer growth
    poles in the southern rimlands on a national scale.

As we look to the future, it is the confluence of
broader national phenomena with the momentum of the city's
historic past that will determine the outlines of New York
as an employment and residential nexus. In this study,
we have projected the structure and composition of New York
City's population, households, and employment through the
year 1985, giving regard to each of the preceding factors.
Operationally, a linked economic-demographic projection
model has been designed, centering about sequential cohort
component analyses, wherein population change is a function of net natural increase and migration. The former
component is predicated on the city's historic (1970)
population profile - partitioned by age, color, and sex -
which is aged (via survival rates) through three five-
year periods. For each time interval, the employment projection provides the basis for determining migration, which
is then used to modify the population distribution at the
end of each period. The major assumption is that employment opportunity, or the lack thereof, is a principle
determinant of population movements. At the end of each
five-year projection interval, after the aged population
is adjusted via migration, births are estimated to
establish the final population levels. The latter are
derived as a function of projected national fertility
patterns, linking the city to the national dynamic. The
employment projections, derived from a separate submodel,
show a substantial diminution of the rate of decline that
characterized the recent past.

1. Total employment in New York is expected to
    stabilize at 3.2 million jobs by 1985, a loss
    of 300,000 jobs over the 1975 to 1985 period.
    The bulk of the losses accrue in the latter
    half of the 1970s.

2. Significantly, government employment, which bul-
warked the city's economy throughout the 1960s,
is projected to account for over one-half of the
job losses. Absent the fiscal crisis, New York
City's employment would stabilize at a somewhat
higher level.

3. The employment losses translate into substantial
negative migration flows. The mismatch between
the supply of labor (drawn from the population
aged for each period) and that required by the
economic base generates a net outmigration of
over 800,000 people from New York between 1975
and 1985.

The population change projected for the city follows
a pattern analogous to that of employment - continued contraction in size but at a rate much abated from that of
the 1970 to 1975 period.

1. The population of New York in 1985 will approach
7.2 million people, down from about 7.5 million
in 1975 and 7.9 million in 1970.

2. With reduced levels of fertility, the gains
secured through net natural increase are not sufficient to counteract the effects of outmigration.

3. The latter will represent a persistent dilemma
for the foreseeable future, even if employment
were to stabilize immediately. During each projection interval, despite a base population depleted through the migration of the preceding
period, the natural aging of the population results in an increasing number of individuals in
their working-age years. As the potential supply
of labor keeps exceeding the labor force demand,
further impetus to outmigration is sustained.

4. While labor force pressures are conventionally
conceived as being eased by the coming of age
of the baby bust cohorts, the total size of the
labor force will continue to increase, at least
through 1985. While the number of new entrants
will certainly decrease, their absolute magnitude
is greater than that of the older cohorts exiting
from the labor force.

5. At the same time, nonwhites are projected to represent 50 percent of the city's total population
by 1985, a consequence both of white outmigration
and the lower fertility rates of whites.

6. The great bulk of the population in 1985 - 2.8
million out of 7.2 million people - will be concentrated in the 25-to 44-years-of-age sectors,
into which the baby boom cohorts will have
matured. The number of individuals below 14 years
of age and above 45 years of age will have con-
tracted significantly.

The city will have lost over 660,000 people between
1970 and 1985, but many of the consequences of population
decline will be mitigated by the city's linkage to
another national transformation - the changing size and
configuration of America's household.

1. Nationally, primary individual households -
singles or two or more unrelated individuals -
are the fastest growing living arrangement; traditional husband-wife families the slowest.

2. Reflecting this development, as well as that of
declining rates of fertility, is the long-term
shrinkage in size o the American household.
A surge in household formations has been projected
nationally. Between 1975 and 1985 the number of
households is expected to increase by almost
one-quarter.

3. New York City has been at the frontier of this
evolution, evidencing households consistently
smaller than those of the rest of the nation,
and a marked skew toward "atypical" households.

4. As these tendencies persist in the future, our
projections indicate considerable growth in the
number of households and in housing demand in
New York City. Despite continued population
declines, the city will secure over 200,000 additional households between 1975 and 1985, an increase from 2.86 million to over 3 million
households.

5. Virtually all of these gains in the number of
households are accounted for by the baby boom
generation - the bulk of the additional household
heads will be between 25 and 44 years of age.
And, the emerging formats will be dominated by

primary individual households. <u>As a result,
the demand for housing will not abate, but
increase</u>, even as the total population undergoes
a long term decline.

These projections must be viewed as a series of
future expectations based upon very specific conditions
and assumptions; they are not to be considered unconstrained
forecasts. They will reflect future reality only to the
degree that the linkages and relationships we have specified remain valid and operative over the next decade.
Consequently, our projections represent one possible
developmental track of New York City's continuing economic
and demographic evolution. The overall study defines a
set of future parameters - a number of leverage points -
giving the city an opportunity to alter the projected
course of events. At the same time, however, some of the
forces and trends in effect are of such fixed momentum
and inertia as to be virtually immune to deflection.
Consequently, the basic tendencies that are projected are
probably correct in pattern and direction; their precise
scale and magnitude are subject to somewhat more uncertainty. A fuller description of the summary of findings
follows.

SUMMARY OF FINDINGS

Historic local trends and relationships provide the
initial basis for future expectations. They are, however,
modified and constrained by the broader patterns of change
affecting the nation as a whole. The economic trendlines,
and their spatial implications, are of vital importance
in this regard.

THE BROADER SETTING OF ECONOMIC CHANGE

The 1970s are turning into a decade of challenge for
many longstanding convictions. The chain of aging central cities - the centerpieces of industrial urbanization -
stretching from Boston to St. Louis has been enveloped
by a sweep of events that would bewilder a transplanted
urban observer of the 1960s. The traditional bases of
industrial America have become prisoners of their earlier
history and are experiencing the dislocations caused by
accelerating technological change, a maturing economy,
and an increasingly mobile and footloose population. It
has become impossible to evaluate the concerns of New
York City without reference to the broader regional
dimension, which manifests the long-term maturation of the
nation's social and economic parameters.

1. A very powerful momentum has built up over the
past fifteen years, sweeping employment and
population growth away from the older metropolitan
centers of the Northeast and North Central states
to the newer growth poles of the South and West.
The "rise of the Sunbelt" and the "decline of
the Northeast", while becoming standard articles
of media discourse and staples of political
rhetoric, are realities firmly documented in the
nation's social and economic data.

2. From 1960 to 1975, the period we consider as the
long-term trend of recent history, total employment growth has increasingly bypassed New York
City's immediate environments.

Total Employment Change: 1960 to 1975

	Percent Change
U.S. Total	46.6
Northeast Region	21.7
Middle Atlantic Division	18.7
North Central Region	36.2
South Region	69.9
West Region	69.5

The Middle Atlantic Division, comprising New York,
New Jersey, and Pennsylvania, is the weakest per-
former within the nation's most laggard region.

3. The short-term trend is gauged by the data of the
1970 to 1975 period, the patterns of which persist unabated through August of 1977, the last
statistical benchmark before the termination of
this study. There is a marked acceleration in
scale of the tendencies isolated over the longer
term period.

Total Employment Change: 1970 to 1975

	Percent Change
U.S. Total	8.5
Northeast Region	- 0.2
Middle Atlantic Division	- 1.6
North Central Region	4.4
South Region	16.4
West Region	15.8

The slower national growth context has exacerbated the problems of New York City's regional
and divisional settings. While the post-1975
national recovery has eased the difficulties
somewhat, the longer term readjustments have
not been altered to any appreciable extent.

4. The economies of the Northeast and North Central
   Regions have historically been based upon manufacturing, as befits the older industrial heartland of America. The spatial shifts of manufacturing underpin the dynamics of total employment change over the 1960 to 1975 period.

Manufacturing Employment Change: 1960 to 1975

                                        Percent Change

U.S. Total   8.8
Northeast Region   -13.9
  Middle Atlantic Division   -15.0
North Central Region   - 4.2
South Region   41.0
West Region   17.8

The locus of manufacturing activity is undergoing
a fundamental transformation.

5. Again, the short-term trend (1970 to 1975) docu-
   ments an increase in the pace of change. As the
   United States is cast in the role of capitalism's
   last hope in the international arena, so too is
   the Sunbelt similarly envisioned within the
   national framework. In a period of overall
   manufacturing stagnation, the contraction within
   the Northeast is particularly ominous.

Manufacturing Employment Change: 1970 to 1975

                                        Percent Change

U.S. Total   - 7.4
Northeast Region   -16.2
  Middle Atlantic Division   -17.0
North Central Region   - 9.1
South Region   0.5
West Region   1.1

The question raised by these growth disparities
concerns the degree to which the overall experience of the Northeast Region and Middle

Atlantic Division is a function of the "writing off" of obsolete industrial infrastructures from the inventory of operational and competitive means of production.

6. Manufacturing - goods production functions - has traditionally been viewed as export oriented, relating to markets and competitive situations much broader than immediate local contexts. In contrast, the private nonmanufacturing and govern- mental sectors have generally been considered as service-oriented activities, dependent on local populations. While this distinction has become increasingly blurred as the post-industrial era matures, the latter activities serve as the major growth vehicles for the nation's economy.

7. From 1960 to 1975, the national growth in private nonmanufacturing employment (58.9 percent) far outdistanced that of manufacturing (8.8 percent). Yet, the nonmanufacturing sectors of the Northeast and its constitutent subareas trailed the perfor- mances of these sectors in the balance of the country.

Private Nonmanufacturing Employment Change:
1960 to 1975

	Percent Change
U.S. Total Total	58.9
Northeast Region	36.5
Middle Atlantic Division	30.2
North Central Region	50.6
South Region	77.8
West Region	80.1

As shown in the main body of the study, these disparities are substantially correlated to differential population growth patterns.

8. As the latter have become more accentuated in the short-term time frame, so has nonmanufac- turing employment been affected.

Private Nonmanufacturing Employment Change:
1970 to 1975

U.S. Total	14.3
Northeast Region	5.1
Middle Atlantic Division	3.0
North Central Region	11.1
South Region	22.1
West Region	20.3

9. Total government employment change shows
   narrower interregional differentials. Yet,
   to the degree that the growth in the Northeast
   and North Central Regions is not supported by
   federal transfer payments, the question of fiscal capacity, in the face of lagging private
   economic activity, is raised.

Total Government Employment Change: 1960 to 1975

	Percent Change
U.S. Total	78.1
Northeast Region	66.6
Middle Atlantic Division	67.1
North Central Region	68.3
South Region	87.7
West Region	90.6

10. In the short-term time period (1970 to 1975), the
    gaps are expanding analogously to the other em-
    ployment sectors.

Total Government Employment Change: 1970 to 1975

	Percent Change
U.S. Total	13.6
Northeast Region	13.9
Middle Atlantic Division	12.4
North Central Region	3.3
South Region	20.8
West Region	18.0

11. Included within total government employment is the
    federal civilian subsector, whose economic impact
    may approximate that of a basic (export) industry.
    Over the 1960 to 1975 period, growth has mainly
    been targeted away from New York City's immediate
    settings.

Federal Civilian Employment Change: 1960 to 1975

	Percent Change
U.S. Total	22.4
Northeast Region	3.3
Middle Atlantic Division	3.6
North Central Region	17.3
South Region	31.9
West Region	29.9

12. The situation evolved into actual employment
     withdrawals over the 1970 to 1975 period,
     aggravating the problems attached to a stag-
     nant private sector.

Federal Civilian Employment Change: 1970 to 1975

                                          Percent Change

U. S. Total   1.6
Northeast Region   - 2.5
  Middle Atlantic Division   - 1.5
North Central Region   - 0.2
South Region   3.6
West Region   3.2

13. In summary, New York City is enmeshed in the web
     of a long-term trendline (1960 to 1975) which has
     served to weaken the vitality of the Northeast
     compared to that of the southern and western parts
     of the nation. In the short-term (1970 to 1975)
     a marked amplification of the longer term ten-
     dencies is apparent, with gradual transitions
     supplanted by more abrupt dislocations.

     Before turning to the specifics of New York City's
economic environment, the forces underlying the national
transformation should be briefly reviewed. What has occurred is the product of a number of factors coming together
at a certain time in a unique way, interacting with and
reinforcing one another.

Economic Maturity and Regional Convergence[3] *In the early
stages of a nation's development, regional growth differentials increase as modern industrial technologies are absorbed
by regions and territories endowed either with appropriate
resources, location, or with creative entrepreneurs. As an
economy matures, a process of regional convergence commences -
the latecomers have a backlog of modern technologies to absorb; the older regions must depend on the flow of new
technologies while carrying a heavier load of older industrial plant. Additionally, as regions (the early leaders)
become more affluent, more resources are allocated to lower
productivity services, dampening the potential for continued high rates of growth. The Sunbelt may be the consequence of natural regional evolution and convergence.*

*Aging Capital Plants. The industrial infrastructures of
our older regions and cities relate to production methods
and approaches that are no longer competitive. The shifts
of jobs and the declining shares of capital investment
within these regions indicate that obsolescence is not
being countered effectively.*

Rationalization of Labor Intensive Industries. *A virtual
revolution has occurred in the technologies of goods production, information processing, and communications. While
automation and technological change may possibly produce
new jobs equivalent in number to those replaced, it is
clear that their geographic loci do not necessarily coin-
cide, nor do the skills and work patterns of the individuals
concerned.*

Declining Urban Linkages. *The historic linkage between
manufacturing activity and urban location has been term-
inated as a result of the rationalization of labor intensive industries. America's older cities were predicated on manufacturing industries. The passing of the
golden age of manufacturing - the great industrial transformation - has left us with a number of overgrown
"factory towns."*

Absorption and Locational Decisionmaking. *Older linkages
have also been weakened with the emergence of conglomerates
and multinational corporations absorbing what were previously locally owned firms, perhaps insulating locational
decisionmaking from such subjective factors as historical
ties, i.e., family owned businesses may be loathe to
stray too far from their traditional setting. While
arguments could be made to the contrary, larger scale
organization may imply the increasing economic ration-
ality of locational decisions, with industries becoming
increasingly "footloose."*

The Dissolution of the Industrial Metropolis. *The transition into the post industrial era not only lends question to the rationale of the manufacturing city, but
also to the historic industrial metropolis encompassing
it. New spatial formats of industrial activity are
synthesizing, rendering older configurations obsolete.*

Accelerating Industrial Evolution. *It is apparent that
the growth in service and white collar functions has
not been able to compensate for urban manufacturing
losses. The latter have occurred just as the rationalization and automation of paper and information handling
has finally come to fruition, limiting effective increases in labor force commensurate with increased
levels of activity.*

Hardening of the Arteries. *Aging regions develop a
variety of conflicting property interests in the broader
sense of the term, creating inhibitors that limit their
ability to adapt to new industrial realities, thereby
reducing their desirability for new entrants.*

Hostile Business Environment. As a consequence, the costs of conducting economic activity in the Northeast have reached ominous levels in comparison to the new growth areas. Taxation, unionization, and a long developing antibusiness milieu all impinge upon the locational decisionmaking process.

Spatial Homogenization. Broader technological changes, such as the interstate highway system domestically and dry bulk cargo shipping internationally, undermine the locational advantage once inherent in the Northeast. Similarly, alternative developments, such as the communications revolution, have made heretofore bypassed areas now directly competitive.

Receptivity to Growth. Locational decisionmakers are subject not only to basic economic constraints, but also to subtle, yet vital, interactions with local political structures. And in the growth areas outlined above, receptivity to potential new industrial relocatees is high, in contrast to that of the older settings. The lower business cost package in the South in particular is a specific manifestation of its receptivity to economy activity.

The Enclaves of Private Enterprise. The business community in the broadest of senses may perceive the basic tenets of capitalism as being increasingly under attack from all quarters. According to this thesis, the regional flows of economic activity can be interpreted as strategic withdrawals to enclaves characterized by political ideologies revering private enterprise.

The Federal Expenditure Matrix. The dynamics of federal spending have tended to replicate the pattern of private economic activity flows. Whether they have been channeled in this fashion because of market realities (i.e., federal grants may tend to follow people and jobs) or, conversely, have actually served to structure market forces, is as yet unclear. Whatever the case, they assuredly have aggravated the economic posture of the Northeast.

The Washington-New York City Transformation. The growing regulatory power of the national government has come to dominate many dimensions of American society. The gravitation of the nation's major public and private decisionmaking apparatus to the Washington locus implies the demise of New York City as the capital and headquarters of private enterprise, and contributes significantly to the Northeast's diminished economic stature.

Energy Importation. The Northeast Region depends much
more heavily on petroleum for residential and industrial
uses compared to the Sunbelt, which utilizes far less
expensive natural gas for the bulk of its energy needs.
The Northeast has few indigenous energy resources and
is a major importer. In 1972, $7 billion was spent by
its member states on fuel importation; this total
ballooned to $20.7 billion by 1975.[4] Since the growth
leaders of the 1970s are the energy producing states,
it is clear that the changing energy matrix has contributed significantly to the Northeast's diminished economic posture.

Facilitating Mechanisms. Earlier in this century, the
impetus toward population decentralization - suburbanization - was underlaid by two factors. The first centered
about facilitating mechanisms. The pyramiding of successive technological innovations made feasible the
habitation of territories beyond formal city boundaries.
To cite but one example, the widespread use of air
conditioning has permitted the larger scale equivalent
of suburbanization to occur by equalizing regional
climates.

Social and Cultural Predispositions. A second factor,
basic social desires, must act in conjunction with the
first to produce large scale migrations. The vacation
of settings thought of as undesirable socially or
environmentally for more pristine and/or amenity-rich
alternatives has now been permitted to work itself out
over the entire geography of the nation. Suburban
flight has given way to regional shift.

Complexity vs. Autonomy. The complex infrastructure inherent in the aging industrial metropolises of the
"snowbelt" has become one of their principal liabilities.
As discipline wanes, this state of high interdependence
places individuals in fragile environments susceptible
to external events. Autonomy becomes desirable and is
sought in the less complex more primitive habitats in
the Sunbelt.

The Decline of Agricultural Migration. The past fifteen
years appear to mark the terminal shift of population
as a function of the agricultural revolution. The
dissolution of labor intensive farming has run its course.
The northern metropolises have been relieved of a
significant source of population replenishment.

The Expanding Retirement Vehicle. The elderly and retired
have become a major force in American society. Their
segregation into specialized residential subcommunities

*throughout the Sunbelt has an economic impact approxi-
mating that of a basic (exporting) industry in that
they generate an income flow (pensions and social
security) from territories external to their new refuges.
Moreover, the transfer of their fixed asset positions
represents a net increment in wealth for the growth
regions.*

*The Critical Mass Phenomenon. As the growing concentra-
tions of people and jobs form the support threshold for
the development of "urban" amenities and functions, the
infrastructures of older areas become redundant. The
translation of income flows to new areas fosters the
rapid replication of older facilities, undermining the
economic rationale of the passed-over resources.*

*Shifting Market Loci. The sustained higher growth rates
in the southern and western regions of the country over
the last several decades, as well as the emergence of the
two preceding phenomena, make the Northeast increasingly
distant from the growing markets of America. It is to
these markets that population serving economic activities are linked, and the development of these markets
reinforces the momentum of the overall trendline.*

*Declining Export Functions. The latter factor also trans-
lates into declining export functions for the Northeast
economy, while the South concurrently undergoes "import
substitution." The locational calculus which dictated
the historic concentrations of wealth and economic
activity in the Northeast has been substantially under-
mined; the region may be overdeveloped relative to its
waning export role in the future. Self-sufficiency in
the South implies contraction in the Northeast.*

*Shifting Criteria of Locational Decisionmaking. Gaining
increased significance for locational decisionmaking
are the basic residential preferences of the more important employee subgroups. Select industries have become
"footloose" with the homogenization of the economic
attributes of "place," and respond to their key person-
nel. Hence residential desires, as depicted above,
become a force in themselves for the locational settings
of economic activity.*

The convergence of these forces provides a complex
dynamic enveloping the particulars of New York City and
its regional environment. They set the stage for both
the immediate and longer term future.

NEW YORK CITY EMPLOYMENT CHANGE

The decreasing relative position of the Northeast Region within the national economic hierarchy prescribes limits to the range of future options available to New York City's economy. If the city were embedded in an expanding regional growth context, at least there might be the possibility that it could secure some portion of that expansion. A stagnant setting, however, virtually precludes substantial future growth - stability would tend to define the optimistic scenario.

At the same time, the key to the future of both the region and the city - absent an explicit national growth policy - is the performance of the American economy. Strong national growth will provide a broader range of opportunities for the Northeast, and subsequently for New York City, in comparison to those offered by a weak national economy. Consequently, a considerable portion of the city's destiny will be defined by forces and events external to its boundaries and control.

1. A vigorous national growth context during the 1960s insulated New York City's employment base from the economic declines afflicting other central cities of the Northeast. Between 1960 and 1970, the city's employment total hovered in the vicinity of 4 million jobs. Internally, however, major structural changes were experienced, as the city adapted to the post-industrial transformation and the emerging service era.

   a) Over 190,000 manufacturing jobs were lost, 19.8 percent of the 1960 base.[5] In the immediate post-World War II years, there were over one million manufacturing jobs in New York City. By 1970, the total declined to 776,000 jobs.

   b) Reflecting the increasing critical mass of population (and consumers) in suburbia, which permitted the replication of facilities once unique to the city, the wholesale and retail trade sector also experienced employment declines (106,000 jobs - 11.6 percent of the 1960 base).

   c) At the same time, compensatory growth in other industrial sectors occurred. Finance, insurance, and real estate secured an additional 64,400 jobs

EXHIBIT 1
NEW YORK CITY EMPLOYMENT CHANGE: 1960 TO 1975
(Numbers in thousands)

	1960	1970	1975	Change: 1960 to 1970 Number	Change: 1960 to 1970 Percent	Change: 1970 to 1975 Number	Change: 1970 to 1975 Percent
Total	3,954.1	3,999.1	3,498.9	45.0	1.1	-500.2	-12.5
Mining	2.0	2.0	1.5	0.0	0.0	- 0.5	-25.0
Construction	163.3	130.0	92.0	-33.3	-20.4	- 38.0	-29.2
Manufacturing	967.0	775.8	534.4	-191.2	-19.8	-241.4	-31.1
Transportation and Public Utilities	332.8	334.2	277.5	1.4	0.4	- 56.7	-17.0
Wholesale and Retail Trade	918.0	811.8	695.1	-106.2	-11.6	-116.7	-14.4
Finance, Insurance, and Real Estate	418.7	483.1	443.7	64.4	15.4	- 39.4	- 8.2
Services	744.1	899.4	882.6	155.3	20.9	- 16.8	- 1.9
Government	408.2	562.8	572.1	154.6	37.9	9.3	1.7

Note: Data have been converted from wage and salary employment to total employment.

Source: U.S. Department of Labor, Bureau of Labor Statistics, Employment and Earnings, Washington, D.C.:U.S. Government Printing Office, monthly.

(15.4 percent); services accrued a gain
of 155,300 jobs (20.9 percent); and
government expanded by 154,600 jobs
(37.9 percent). Substitution and change
within the context of overall stability
were characteristic of New York City
throughout the 1960s.

2. When the national economy faltered in the 1970 to
1975 period, and the new regional and energy
realities took hold, a fundamental transition
was produced. The process of change was no longer
compensatory; rather it was one of painful shrinkage.

   a) Total employment fell below 3.5 million
      jobs - over 500,000 jobs were lost, 12.5
      percent of the 1970 base.

   b) Almost half of this decline was attribut-
      able to the manufacturing sector, which
      lost over 241,000 jobs (31.1 percent).
      Manufacturing employment in 1975
      (534,400 jobs) was only 50 percent of
      that in the late 1940s.

   c) The private nonmanufacturing sector could
      not counterbalance this decline. Finance,
      insurance, and real estate lost almost
      39,400 jobs; wholesale and retail trade,
      -116,700 jobs; and services, -16,800 jobs.

   d) And no longer could government employment
      expansion sustain a faltering private
      sector. Only 9,300 additional jobs were
      secured, as state and local growth was
      barely sufficient to offset the with-
      drawals of the federal sector.

   d) Consequently, the conventional wisdom of
      the 1960s - of white collar office jobs
      effectively supplanting their manufac-
      turing counterparts - had been rendered
      obsolete.

3. Over the 1975 to 1977 period, evidence is beginning to mount that the painful process of erosion
is abating. That this is occasioned by a surging
national growth context has not appeared to have
dampened a growing optimism. Nonetheless, the
fiscal crisis has hindered the transition to
stability - the governmental sector lost 84,200
jobs over this period, exerting a considerable

drag on the overall economy.

4. The band of projections through 1985 encompasses
   several possible evolutionary paths. The upper
   boundary defines immediate stability at the 3.5
   million job level, the same as 1975. The lower
   boundary projects continued declines, but at a
   decreasing rate over time. Stability is
   approached, but at a much lower threshold - at
   fewer than 2.9 million jobs.

5. The central projection, however, represents the
   immediate working parameter for the balance of
   the model. It defines a path of slow erosion -
   relative to the 1970 to 1975 experience - with
   the 1985 projection standing at just over 3.2
   million jobs. The bulk of the losses are expected to accrue during the 1975 to 1980 period
   with stability projected for the 1980s.

   a) Consistent with 1975 to 1977 periods,
      but contrary to the 15 previous years,
      the governmental sector is projected
      to decline, accounting for over half of
      the city's losses.

   b) Manufacturing is also expected to decline
      throughout the ten-year projection span,
      but at a rate far less precipitous than
      the recent past.

   c) Significantly, private nonmanufacturing
      employment, while in total reflecting
      stability, will show minimal capacity to
      compensate for the expected losses in
      the manufacturing and governmental sec-
      tors. The job intensive opportunities
      of the post-industrial transformation are
      bypassing New York City.

6. The central projection indicates, then, a transition whose magnitude, though negative, is
   limited, thus permitting the city to effectively
   adjust to its main thrust. While it provides
   little evidence for complacency, it also gives
   little reason for despair. Certainly, the
   potential of public policy inputs yielding
   significant dividends is present. But only if the
   political will is certain.

7. Nonetheless, the path defined by the central projection establishes the estimated magnitude of

EXHIBIT 2
NEW YORK CITY EMPLOYMENT PROJECTIONS: 1975 TO 1985
(Numbers in thousands)

	1975	1980			1985		
		High	Central Projection	Low	High	Central Projection	Low
Total	3,498.9	3,484.4	3,285.9	3,087.0	3,534.6	3,212.6	2,890.6
Mining	1.5	1.7	1.6	1.5	1.7	1.5	1.3
Construction	92.0	87.7	73.7	59.7	93.1	76.9	60.7
Manufacturing	534.4	556.5	514.5	472.5	559.5	475.6	391.7
Transportation and Public Utilities	277.5	280.1	256.7	233.3	283.0	247.8	212.6
Wholesale and Retail Trade	695.1	703.5	663.4	623.3	709.4	644.2	579.0
Finance, Insurance and Real Estate	443.7	464.3	438.1	411.9	491.7	445.0	398.3
Services	882.6	899.1	876.6	853.9	932.8	896.2	859.6
Government	572.1	491.9	461.4	430.9	463.4	425.4	387.4
Federal	91.4	77.8	75.5	73.2	64.4	60.6	56.8
State	47.9	47.9	50.2	52.5	55.6	53.0	50.4
Local	432.8	366.2	335.7	305.2	343.4	311.8	280.2

Note: Data are cast in terms of total employment

Source: CUPR Projections.

New York City's resident employment - employed
New York City residents, working both inside
and outside the city.

Year	Employment Level	Resident Employment Demand
1970	3,999,100	3,202,906
1975	3,498,900	2,885,997
1980	3,285,900	2,790,694
1985	3,212,600	2,781,472

However, according to the premise of the projection model, to the degree that the labor force
supply (employed plus unemployed) exceeds the
demands of the city's employment base, outmigration, both of the work force and its dependents,
will be stimulated. As we shift to the analysis
of population, the aging of the base population
implies an increase in the number of people in
their working-age years, through 1985, setting
the stage for population outflows.

POPULATION

While labor force demand generally declines, there
is a general demographic force over the 1970 to 1985
period continually replenishing and increasing the population of labor force age. Only after 1985 does this
growth diminish appreciably. The situation is made apparent by comparing the actual projected population between the ages of 15 to 64 years - assuming for the purposes of simplicity that this age span encompasses those
of working age[6] - to that which would result if the base
population was aged or survived in place (assuming the
city was a closed system, allowing neither in- nor outmigration).

Year	Projected Population (after migration)	Aged Base Population (closed system - no migration)
July 1, 1970 Base	5,071,708	5,071,708
1975	5,027,168	5,152,114
1980	5,117,745	5,249,998
1985	5,073,520	5,350,357

Without migration, the number of New York City residents of working age would tend to expand throughout the projection interval. However, only through outmigration is the projected population level (and its labor force correlate) kept in balance with the labor force demand of the economic base. The factor is key to understanding the population projections, implying that economic stability in and of itself does not provide the capacity to absorb the labor force expansion.

The Components

The two basic components of population change are migration and net natural increase (births minus deaths). While migration in this study is essentially cast as a residual of employment change, net natural increase - the maturation of the base population - is fundamentally governed by the parameters of the past as they intersect broader national population developments. The city's future population, then, is a prisoner of historical inertia and the momentum of national forces and processes. Both of these concerns define the essential backdrop for evaluating the evolution of New York City's residential base.

The National Context

1. A long-term trend toward decreasing rates of growth is a fundamental characteristic of the nation's population and is primarily the result of sustained fertility rate declines experienced over the past 20 years.

2. Fertility rate changes over the past half century have also resulted in major age-structure patterns that have dominated the nation's population shifts in the recent past and whose implications are basic to the future. The principle patterns are encompassed by two phenomena, the baby boom and baby bust, which have been and will continue to be reflected in New York City.

3. The baby boom was initiated in 1946 by a sharp increase in the number of births, a trend which continued through 1957, the peak of the postwar era. Approximately 47 million children were born over this 12 year period, creating a permanent but moving bulge in the nation's age profile.

4. As this group aged, it flooded the nation's school systems in the 1950s and 1960s, its higher educational systems in the 1960 and 1970s, and its housing and job markets in the 1970s and early 1980s. The latter is of prime significance to New York City as the bulge shifts into the 25 to 44 years of age sectors over the 1975 to 1985 period.

5. The subsequent baby bust is foreordained to trail the wake of the baby boom tide as it matures through the country's age structure. A consequence of declining fertility rates, the baby bust cohorts impact the under-14-years-of-age sector through 1980 and, subsequently, the 15-to-24-years-of-age category. While raising the dilemmas of contraction to new prominence, the overall phenomenon, as will be shown in household configurations, is significant in terms of the declining relative importance of family-raising households. As the necessity for suburban childrearing environments wanes, areas such as New York City are presented with perhaps unique opportunities.

6. And, despite the baby bust, the national population of working age (defined as between 15 to 64 years of age for purposes of simplicity) will increase from 125.2 million to 153.9 million people over the 1970 to 1985 period, a rate of growth far exceeding that of total population. Even ignoring the increasing labor force participation rates for women, the pressures on the job market will ease only slightly through 1985. As this eventuality permeates down to the scale of New York City, even a stabilized local economy would not prove sufficient to mitigate the city's unemployment and outmigration dilemmas.

New York City: The Recent Past

In the recent past, New York City has closely reflected national population trendlines, while also exhibiting its own unique attributes.

1. *While the population of the United States increased by 13.3 percent from 1960 to 1970, that of New York increased by only 1.5 percent. The city's white population declined by 8.9 percent (591,821 people), but was compensated by a nonwhite increase of 61.7 percent (704,699).*

2. *The only white age groups within the city to show positive gains were the 15-to-24-years-of-age group (into which the baby boom cohort had aged by 1970) and the elderly, those 65 years of age and over. The nonwhite population demonstrated increases throughout the age continuum, but the gains were greater in the more youthful age sectors.*

3. *Although New York City had a net outmigration of 497,283 individuals, the net natural increase (610,161) was sufficient for the city to register a population increase in total.*

4. *The migrational experience was dominated by the following patterns:*

    a. *The overall city migration total was a consequence of a white net outmigration of 882,516 people and a nonwhite net inmigration of 385,233 people.*

    b. *The white outmigration cut across all of its component age sectors (when defined by 10 year intervals). However, the major losses encompassed those age groups which can be inferred to represent households in the childbearing stage of the family life cycle, as well as the elderly (65 years of age and over). However, further age and sex disaggregations did reveal the presence of positive migration segments - young individuals in their 20s probably not in the process of childbearing.*

    c. *The vacating of the city by white family-raising households was paralleled by the inmigration of their nonwhite counterparts. The latter represented the major portion of nonwhite inmigration, which was represented in all age groups.*

5. *The city's net natural increase, the consequence of births in conjunction with the aging of its base population, reflected both broader national trends and the age structure of the population of the base period.*

    a. *The pattern of white net natural increase exactly paralleled that of the city as a whole. Declines were evident*

*in the age groups of under five years
and between 25 and 54 years of age.
The latter was a consequence of the
low birth rates of the Depression and
World War II era, as well as the aging
of those cohorts depleted by the earlier
suburbanization flows of the 1950 to 1960
period. Positive increases were registered in the ranks of the elderly and those
age sectors into which the baby boom bulge
had aged.*

b. *The nonwhite population exhibited sharp
gains through the process of net natural
increase in all age sectors except in the
25 to 34 year old (which declined) and the
35 to 44 year old (which showed a minimal
gain) groups. Again, in 1970 these age
ranges reflect the historic birth rate
declines of the 1930s and early 1940s.*

6. *The overall age-structure changes within New York
City generally mirrored those changes taking place
at the national scale.*

The 1970 to 1975 Period

The shifts in New York City's population over the
1970 to 1975 period - as those of its economic base -
appear unprecedented in modern historical annals. However, it is not the shape and pattern of change that are
surprising, but its severity. Its outlines could
have been perceived from the evidence of the previous
decade; its scale of import could not.

1. *In the 1970 to 1975 period, the city's population
is projected to have fallen from 7,893,551 to
7,490,690, a loss of 402,861 people or 5.1
percent.*

2. *The only age specific subpopulations that demonstrate growth are the correlates of the
baby boom cohorts for this time period - the 15-
to 34-years-of-age sectors. All other age
groups of the total population show declines,
with the major losses attached to the age
sectors spawned in periods of low fertility -
the baby bust generation (under 14 years of
age) and the Depression era progeny (35 to
44 years of age).*

EXHIBIT 3
NEW YORK CITY POPULATION
BY AGE: 1970 TO 1985

Age Category	1970	1975	1980	1985
Total	7,893,551	7,490,690	7,391,510	7,231,198
< 5	613,738	496,813	519,854	527,984
5-14	1,257,374	1,041,381	832,302	742,535
15-24	1,258,373	1,296,348	1,273,863	1,084,822
25-34	1,075,505	1,347,501	1,568,478	1,620,530
35-44	911,264	771,696	875,558	1,163,284
45-54	937,952	839,820	701,291	585,808
55-64	888,614	771,803	698,555	619,076
65+	950,731	925,328	921,609	889,159

Source: CUPR Projections.

3. When the city's population is segmented into
white/nonwhite categories, the complexity underlying the city's transition is emphasized. The
overall decline is the end result of white losses
(-905,361 individuals) in the face of insufficient nonwhite growth (502,500 people).

4. The changing age structure of the white population generally mirrors the overall city pattern.
Gains were secured only by the 25-to 34-years-of-
age sector. In marked contrast, every nonwhite
age group manifested positive growth increments.

5. Other elements of the overall city experience are
revealed by the components of population change -
migration and net natural increase.

   a) The city suffers a net migration loss
   of 576,656 individuals, which cuts
   across all age sectors, except those between 15 and 34 years of age. However,
   the white/nonwhite migration flows diverge. The former shows a net outmigration of 935,439 people while the latter
   experiences a net inmigration of 358,783
   individuals. The white outflow is again
   spearheaded by what we infer to be
   family-raising households; the nonwhite
   inflow by young individuals under 35
   years of age.

   b) The total net natural increase (173,795)
   falls far short of countering the total
   migration loss. For the city as a whole,
   and the white sector, the only age
   groups showing positive natural increase
   components are the 25 to 34 (the maturing
   baby boom residuals) and the over 64
   years-of-age categories. Positive
   gains characterize the nonwhite age structure, excepting only the 5-to 14-years-
   of-age sector (which encompasses the baby
   bust cohort).

6. These changes bear the imprint not only of historical momentum, but also of forces evidenced
on a national scale. The New York City experience
of the 1970 to 1975 period - in terms of age-
structure shifts - generally corresponds to the
national pattern; yet the age-specific changes
are much more pronounced in the city.

The 1975 to 1980 Period

A dampening and gradual abatement in the severity of the early 1970s trendlines is the dominant theme of the 1975 to 1980 period. Yet the city is still enmeshed in the throes of change in its demographic matrix.

1. *The population level of the city falls from 7,480,690 in 1975 to 7,391,510 in 1980, a decline of 99,180 people or 1.3 percent. The age sectors that maintain growth tend to be somewhat older than their counterparts of the preceding period (25 to 44 years of age versus 15 to 34 years of age), underscoring the aging of the baby boom generation. And, as a derivative of the latter, an increase in the under-5-years-of-age population occurs - all other age sectors are characterized by declines.*

2. *Underlying the overall city experience is its white/nonwhite composition.*

   a) *The white sector loses 698,847 individuals (-13.6 percent) as its total falls to the 4.4 million person level. The maturing baby boom cohorts provide the only relief from pervasive declines across the age profile.*

   b) *The nonwhite population increase (599,667 people) fails to offset the white decline. Nonetheless, by 1980, nonwhites comprise 40.1 percent of the city's population, as compared to 31.6 percent in 1975. The gains are registered across the entire nonwhite age spectrum.*

3. *The white/nonwhite transition during this period is underscored by the patterns of migration. The city's total migration (-366,982 people) is the result of a net outflow of 783,409 whites and a net inflow of 416,427 nonwhites. These conflicting movements are representative of the experience of virtually every age group of the respective subpopulations.*

4. *While the overall migration total of the 1975 to 1980 period (-366,982) is considerably smaller than that projected for the preceding five years (-576,656), the net natural increase secured during the 1975 to 1980 period (267,802) is greater than that experienced from 1970 to 1975*

(173,795). Yet the gap between the two compo-
nents remains, defined by continued absolute
population losses for the city.

    a) The white natural increase is attributed
    to the surviving populations bolstering
    the ranks of elderly (65 years of age
    and over), the inertia of the baby boom
    (25 to 44 years of age), and the wave of
    derivative births (under 5 years of age).
    This pattern is analogous to that dis-
    played by the city's population in total.

    b) The total white net natural increase
    (84,562) stands in marked contrast to
    that of nonwhites (183,240).

5. *General correspondence to the projected*
national age-structure changes is again evi-
dent. The major differences are the conse-
quence of the evolution of past variations
(the city's traditional losses among its more
mature citizenry) and the pyramiding effect of
more recent developments - the positive growth
in the city's under-5-years-of-age population
due to the increasing critical mass of the
nonwhite population.

The 1980 to 1985 Period

    The abated levels of population decline of the
1975 to 1980 period served as a brief interlude presag-
ing the greater losses projected between 1980 and 1985.
However, the latter still do not approach in scale the
traumatic events of the 1970 to 1975 era. Additionally,
the experience of the 1980 to 1985 period adds emphasis
to a phenomenon often obscured. While the rate of
economic decline is the smallest of any projection
period, the pace at which the labor force expands maintains the impetus toward outmigration, which in turn
drains the city of valuable population resources.

1. *From 1980 to 1985, the city's projected popu-*
lation losses (160,312 people) draw the over-
all total down to the 7.2 million person
level. The nonwhite population increase
(590,595) is outweighed by white losses
(-750,907). Within the latter subpopulation,
the only age sector to experience growth is
the 35-to 44-years-of-age sector, into which
the leading edge of the baby boom has moved.

2. *The nonwhite population gains virtual parity
   in terms of proportional representation (49.2
   percent). In those age sectors under 25
   years of age, the nonwhite dominance is pronounced. In the more mature age spans, whites
   are still in the majority.*

3. *The projected increase in outmigration (-450,812)
   is the result of the phenomenon discussed above.
   However, the total masks the unrelenting pace
   of white outmigration (-830,720) which exceeds
   the replacement capacity of the nonwhite inflow (379,980).*

4. *The translation of migration losses into absolute population decline is partially buffered
   by the growing size of the net natural increase
   component (290,500). Increasingly, however, the
   latter is weighted toward the nonwhite sector -
   210,687 nonwhites as against 79,813 whites.*

5. *Comparisons between the projected age structure
   of the nation with that of the city show New
   York having a much greater proportion of its
   population falling between the ages of 25 to 44
   years. The 1980 to 1985 changes projected for
   each area show similar patterns, but somewhat
   divergent magnitudes.*

HOUSEHOLD IMPLICATIONS

Population decline implies many painful readjustments in the broad fabric of New York City. However,
in a number of cases, the impacts of population shrinkage will be mitigated by actual increases in the number
of households. Between 1970 and 1985 the following
changes in New York's households, in relation to their
population counterparts, are projected.[7]

Year	Population	Households
1970 (April 1)	7,894,862	2,836,872
1975 (July 1)	7,490,690	2,857,176
1980 (July 1)	7,391,510	2,981,649
1985 (July 1)	7,231,198	3,086,315

1. The evolution of the nation's household configurations maintains the pace of change
   evidenced by its economic and population parameters. While the latter have tended to
   evolve to the general disadvantage of New

York City, the household transformation appears to be a more favorable development.
The trend toward smaller sizes and configurations may serve to bolster the demand for
housing at a time when absolute population declines may be impossible to avert.

2. Over the last intercensal period (1960 to 1970),
   the average household size in the United States
   has declined from 3.33 to 3.14 persons. At
   the same time, New York City's average size of
   household has shifted from 2.88 to 2.74 persons.

3. These changes document a long-term national
   trend toward smaller households. New York City
   is at the leading edge of this evolution.

4. Smaller households and rapid rates of household
   formation imply a demand for housing far in
   excess of that indicated by population growth
   alone. From 1970 to 1976, the number of households in the nation increased from 63.4 million
   to 72.9 million, a growth rate of 14.9 percent.
   At the same time, the nation's population increased by 5.2 percent. This differential between these growth rates has widened over time.

5. By 1976, the average national household size
   had declined to 2.89 persons. The reduced level
   of fertility, soaring divorce rates, and declining marriage rates are all significant in
   this regard. As a result, traditional husband-
   wife families are the nation's slowest growing
   household type. The fastest growing are primary individual households, either single
   persons living alone or with nonrelatives present. Again, as reflected by household size,
   New York City's skew toward more "nontraditional"
   families is more accentuated than that of the
   nation.

6. The national projections portend a surge in
   household formations. Between 1975 and 1985,
   the number of households in the United States
   are projected to increase from 71.8 million to
   88.5 million, a gain of almost one-quarter
   (23.5 percent) over a ten-year span.

7. As a result of the events and forces in motion,
   the number of households in New York City also
   will show considerable growth through 1985,

EXHIBIT 4
NUMBER OF HOUSEHOLDS BY AGE OF THE HEAD OF HOUSEHOLD
NEW YORK CITY: 1975 AND 1985

Age	1975 Number	1975 Percent	1985 Number	1985 Percent
Under 24	199,268	7.0	200,740	6.5
25-34	691,942	24.2	896,801	29.1
35-44	420,266	14.7	658,535	21.3
45-64	932,485	32.6	714,496	23.2
65+	613,215	21.5	615,743	20.0
Total	2,857,176	100.0	3,086,315	100.0

HOUSEHOLD CONFIGURATIONS
NEW YORK CITY: 1975 AND 1985

	1975 Number	1975 Percent	1985 Number	1985 Percent
Household Type				
Total Households	2,857,176	100.0	3,086,315	100.0
Primary Families	1,987,650	69.6	2,032,030	65.9
Husband-Wife	1,520,741	53.2	1,520,936	49.3
Other Male Head	78,580	2.8	79,936	2.6
Other Female Head	388,329	13.6	431,158	14.0
Primary Individuals	986,526	30.4	1,054,285	34.1

Notes: Percents may not add due to rounding.

Source: CUPR Projections.

despite the projection of continued population
declines. Between 1975 and 1985, the city's
resident households will increase from 2.86
million to 3.09 million - the city will secure
almost 230,000 additional households at the
same time as its population losses approach
260,000 people.

8. Virtually all of the household gains of New York
   City, and the bulk of those of the nation, are
   the province of the 25-to 44-years-of-age sectors,
   into which the baby boom matures by 1985.

9. The emerging formats will be dominated by primary
   individual households, composed of either a
   single individual or two or more unrelated individuals, while the traditional husband-wife
   family will decline in both relative and absolute
   terms. Both New York City and the nation will be
   characterized by the ascension of atypical household types.

10. Gauging this transformation is the continued con-
    traction in the average size of both the nation's
    and the city's households. The city's households
    will still reflect historic differentials - a
    skew toward smaller sizes - but the gap between
    the two narrows through the projection interval.

PROJECTIONS AND PUBLIC POLICY

Historic trends and relationships provide the foundation for the future - at a minimum, they establish an
initial base for extrapolation. But they should not be
mistaken for inexorable destiny. The projection methodology of this study, for example, has as its premise
patterns of employment change and their linkage to the
established inertia of the city's population base. It
is the evolution of the historic relationships between
the number of jobs in the city, the proportion of those
jobs held by the resident population, and the ratio between employed and dependent residents which serve, among
others, as basic parameters for the approach. Clearly,
there are an enormous number of variables which could
alter the projected developments. A number of them
(a far from exhaustive list) are discussed below:

1. Welfare Policy. The issue of whether migration
   has been influenced by variations in local welfare policies is a much debated one. Clearly,

however, there do exist as of this writing very
significant gaps between welfare provisions in
many of the states of the South and those of
New York.[8] Would some form of national welfare
administration and benefit equalization alter
future migration, or for that matter occasion
some measure of return of nonwhites from North
to South? While the full impact of such measures
is at best unclear, they may well retard migration
from the South to the nation's major cities, New
York included.

2. Employment Opportunities for Black in the South.
Much of the South's economic revitalization has
bypassed the black delta areas and instead has
been concentrated in the white hill towns;[9]while
economic conditions for nonwhites have improved,
they have not been proportionate to the rejuve-
nation of the area as a whole. Even given these
limitations, there are post-1970 Census Bureau
estimates that indicate some slight measure of
net outmigration of blacks from the North and a
nearly equivalent growth in inmigration to the
South.[10] The substantial efforts on the part of
northeastern states and cities to secure a
greater measure of federal investment in job
opportunities to correct their levels of unemployment are growing. But it is interesting to
speculate as to whether a full systems orienta-
tion, which assumes that migration is a function
of job growth, would indicate that southern
growth has as much, or nearly as much, payoff
for the North as direct investment there, at
least in terms of dependency ratios.

        It is clear, however, that the changing
pattern of racial mores, betokened by the comparative success in school integration and the
like, make the South a more hospitable environment for nonwhites than was hitherto the case.
The relative allure of the North and New York
specifically, therefore, may very well decline,
and with it the pattern of net nonwhite inmigration. It would be highly dubious, at least
in the shortrun, whether this would occasion any
significant level of outmigration.

3. Children of School Age. In the age-specific
migration patterns that have been observed both
historically and which are projected in this
study, there has been a clear linkage between

outmigration of children of school age and their
parents. The phenomenon is one so very frequently noted as to be practically a modular
concept - pre-child-bearing couples living in
the city, then outmigrating as a function of
having children. In this new age - which has
been heralded as an era of childless couples,
or at most very small families, particularly
among whites - the pressures for suburban school
facilities may be far less stringent than has
heretofore been the case, with the demerits of
the city school system, whether real or supposed,
much less significant. As is noted in an adja-
cent study of demographic characteristics of
occupants of loft conversions and 421 structures,
there is a very imposing skew toward enthusiastic
occupancy by the nonchildrearing couple.[11] To
the degree that households of this format expand
in number at a significant rate, the pattern of
white outmigration, particularly in the age
cohorts most susceptible to the allure of "better"
schools, may be much abated. Older age at
marriage, much older age at first child, and
growth of childlessness all may lead not merely
to an enlargement of the white cohorts attracted
to the city, but also to their retention by the
city.

4. Competitive Cost Postures. The development of
central city alternatives to suburban allures
are particularly potent in an era in which the
costs of leaving the city are ever increasing.
The subject of new single-family housing costs
has been studied most intensively; the ratio
between median-income levels and the costs of
housing have degenerated over time. Even more
striking is the problem of high carrying costs,
not only in mortgages but in energy costs, both
directly for homes and for transportation, which
are an essential auxilliary of non-central-city
living. The opportunities of developing urban
alternatives are most substantial and the competitive environment never more favorable.

5. Whites as a Conscious Minority. Achieving suc-
cessful racial integration within New York City
is a contest between the development of an
appropriate package of housing, environment, and
employment incentives on the one hand, and the
migration of population and support structures
as a function of race and class conflict on

the other. Whether suburban, exurban, or region-
ally oriented, the pattern of white outmigration,
particularly of the more affluent, may well
generate self-reinforcing momentum. A decline
in the ratio of whites to nonwhites may in turn
generate an environment that for a variety of
reasons enhances the propensity of whites to
leave.

The pattern of the future, presented here, is not
inexorable. It is rather a baseline projection of the
city's demographic profile, assuming the inertia not only
of present trends, but also of the lack of real effort
within our society at all governmental levels to alter
those lifestyles. A healthy New York is one that provides
opportunity for all, not only the poor or very rich, but
for all. A city of only poor people or of only nonwhite
people will be incapable of serving its constitutents.
What is required is a city of balance in the future. The
costs of not achieving this are evident: the danger of
arriving at that resolution all too clearly stated by
the projections. The issues of action will not wait.

Notes

1. Our projection for 1975, and the components of change over the 1970 to 1975 period, are in substantial agreement with those estimated by the Census Bureau, See: U.S. Bureau of the Census, Current Population Reports Series P-26, No. 76-32, "Estimates of the Population of New York Counties and Metropolitan Areas: July 1, 1975 (Revised) and 1975 (Provisional)," U.S. Government Printing Office, Washington, D.C., August 1977.

2. The conventional employment reporting system of the U.S. Bureau of Labor Statistics is cast in terms of wage and salary (payroll) employment, excluding self-employed and unpaid family workers. In this summary, we have used total employment, including our estimates of self-employed and unpaid family workers. Consequently, there may be some inconsistencies between the numbers presented here and their payroll equivalents used in other reports on the city's economy.

3. The regional convergence hypothesis is that of W.W. Rostow. See: W.W. Rostow, "Regional Development in the United States," in George Sternlieb and James W. Hughes, eds., Revitalizing the Northeast: Prelude to an Agenda (New Brunswick, N.J.: Rutgers University, Center for Urban Policy Research, 1978).

4. The energy costs have been secured from the contribution of the proposed Mid-Atlantic Regional Commission, "Energy Realities," to the preceding volume.

5. Again it should be stressed that the employment numbers represent total jobs and not simply wage and salary (payroll) employment.

6. To maintain consistency with the major data presentations of this study, we have equated the 15-to 64-years-of-age group to that encompassed by the labor force. In the actual computational scheme of the model, 16 years of age is used as the lower boundary, the one conventionally employed for labor force delineations. The upper limit, 64 years of age, has been used because the elderly - 65 years of age and over - are treated as a separate submodel. The operational procedures are detailed in Chapter 1.

7. The population projections correspond quite closely to those of the New York State Economic Development Board, although our household projections are higher

for 1980 and 1985. See: New York State Statistical Yearbook (Albany: New York State Division of the Budget, 1977), pp. 61-62.

8. See Sar A. Levitan, "Welfare Dilemmas," in Sternlieb and Hughes, op.cit.

9. See: Wilbur Thompson, "Economic Processes and Employment Problems in Declining Metropolitan Areas," in George Sternlieb and James W. Hughes, eds., Post-Industrial America: Metropolitan Decline and Inter-Regional Job Shifts (New Brunswick, N.J.: Rutgers University, Center for Urban Policy Research, 1976).

10. See: Vincent P. Barabba, "The National Setting: Regional Shifts, Metropolitan Decline and Urban Decay," ibid.

11. Center for Urban Policy Research, (forthcoming).

Chapter 1

METHODOLOGY: ECONOMIC AND DEMOGRAPHIC PROJECTION

INTRODUCTION

There is a substantial inventory of projection techniques and models for estimating the future growth and decline of populations, as well as changes in their internal composition over time.[1] These span a continuum ranging from the naive - the simple extrapolation of past trends of growth into the future - to more complex elaborations which attempt to model the causal determinants of population change. While the latter seem infinitely preferable to the former, it must be noted that overcomplexity can breed in itself challenges to operational validity. Attempts to model dynamic interacting factors may fall prey to data base limitations, restricting the derivation of empirical linkages, and inhibiting the calibration of theoretically specified relationships. The subsequent imposition of surrogate assumptions - reluctantly fabricated adjustments made to compensate for data limitations - has the potential to undermine the supposed advantages of complex models, placing their results on the same level of validity as that of simple extrapolations.

Such tensions across the modeling framework, however, are not unique to population studies, but are general to all quantitative investigations of social and economic phenomena. Nevertheless, intermediate approaches are possible, attempting to directly incorporate those factors considered to causally underlie the process of change, but only to the degree they are amenable both to data base resources and to time and economic limitations. This is the developmental option implemented in this study with efforts concentrated on

those model incorporations which not only promise to replicate reality, but also offer the potential to improve
operational results.

A major assumption of this linked economic-demographic forecasting model is that economic change stimu-
lates the movement of people. The major question of a
direct causal relationship between employment and migration is left unanswered, but previous empirical studies
have indicated that the two phenomena are highly correlated and there is a mutual interaction between migration and the demand for labor.[2] Operationally, the procedure employed in this study is to project net migration to and from New York City on the basis of
independent projections of employment activity and its
derivatives.[3] Migration is subsequently entered into
the population analysis to interact with the other
components of population change.

The following section presents the overall model
design, displaying and describing its major analytical
procedures. The central feature of the presentation is
a graphic description of the model, to which the
accompanying text discussions are numerically keyed.
The second section isolates the employment sector of
the model and more fully elaborates its major projection components. The final section makes explicit the
major assumptions, premises, and limitations of the
overall model design so that the actual projection results can be placed in a proper evaluative context.

THE OVERALL MODEL

The population projection methodology encompasses
what is conventionally labeled the cohort-component
method or cohort-survival analysis, and is premised on
the recognition that population change is a function of
natural increase and migration. These components are
usually modeled by the following expression:[4]

$$P_{t+n} = P_t + N + M$$

where: P_{t+n} = future population at
                  time t+n

        P_t = initial base population
                  at time t

N = net natural increase (births minus deaths)

M = net migration (inmigration minus outmigration)

The term "cohort" indicates that the analytical procedure is applied to age categories (rather than gross population totals), with the identity of each age group retained as it is carried forward through time.[5] For example, the 1975 cohort comprising population 15 to 19 years of age is projected to 1980 by accounting for deaths (employing survival rates) and migration, at which time the cohort's population will be between 20 and 24 years of age. In this study, the cohorts span five years and define the age profiles of four subpopulations - the male and female sectors of the white and nonwhite populations. In order to retain the identity of the age cohorts, the projection periods must be similar to, or multiples of, the width (in years) of the age groups.

Cohort component analysis is the descriptive term for describing the overall analytical process. In considering the natural increase component (particularly the survival analysis), the cohort-survival terminology is often employed. Algebraically, this portion of the analysis, focusing on the age cohort delineated above, would be defined as

$$_{20\text{-}24}P_{1980} = \left[_{15\text{-}19}S_{1975\text{-}1980} \right] \left[_{15\text{-}19}P_{1975} \right]$$

where: S is the age-specific survival rate

The migrational component of the model is derived from the output of the employment projection series - the assumption is that changes in employment levels will be reflected by (or will simulate) the in- or outmigration of the labor force. Operationally, employment levels are translated into labor force demand (LFD) for each projection period, and are compared to the surviving labor force supply (LFS) - that portion of the survived population estimated to be members of the labor force. The residual of these two independent projections is assumed to represent labor force migration - i.e., the supply and demand sectors will interact to generate population movements - which in turn is pyramided to total population migration. (The migration of the elderly is calculated by a separate submodel.)

EXHIBIT 1-1
MODEL FLOW DIAGRAM

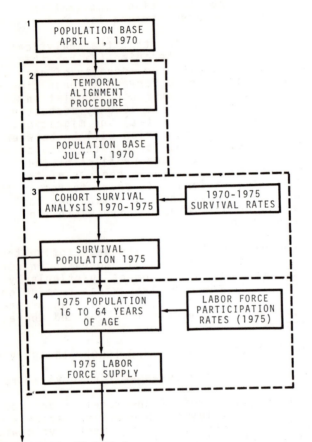

TO STEP 10   TO STEP 6

(Continued)

EXHIBIT 1-1 (continued)
MODEL FLOW DIAGRAM

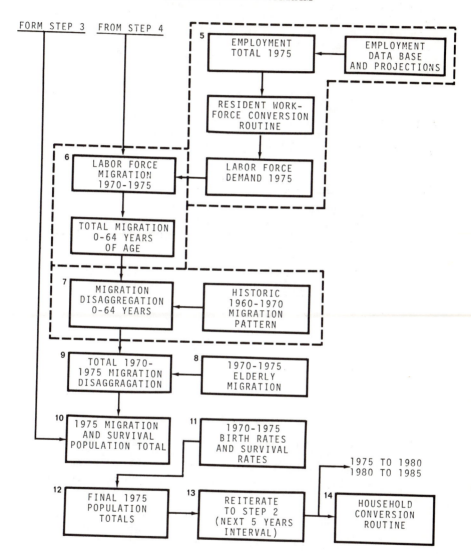

Age and color specific birth rates are subsequently applied to the survived populations after the latter have been adjusted by the migrational components. The resulting births are entered as new cohorts into the population profiles, establishing the final projection for the period in question. The latter, in turn, serves as the base for the succeeding projection interval.

Exhibit 1 provides the flow diagram of the overall projection model, with the numbers corresponding to the major computational procedures (or submodels). The following sections, keyed to the exhibit numbers, elaborate the overall analytical process.

Population Data Base

1. New York City's April 1, 1970 population was partitioned into white/nonwhite and male/female sectors, each disaggregated by five-year age categories.

	White		Nonwhite	
Age	Male	Female	Male	Female
<5				
5-9				
10-14				
.				
.				
.				
.				
65+				

This basic matrix comprises 52 distinct age cohorts (4 X 13) -- four population subgroups defined by 13 age sectors. All succeeding analyses and calculations are operationalized to the level of detail of the basic data input.

2. The July 1, 1970 population matrix (defined by the above format) was extrapolated from the April 1 base by the following formula (temporal alignment procedure):

$$P_x^{7/1/70} = (f_1 P_x^{4/1/70}) - (f_2 P_x^{4/1/60})$$

where: P_x stands for the population of any age category, x for the dates indicated by the superscripts, and f_1 and f_2 are state - specific factors provided in:

Richard Irwin, <u>Guide for Local Area Population Projections</u>, U.S. Bureau of the Census Technical Paper No. 39 (Washington, D.C.: U.S. Government Printing Office, July 1977).

<u>The Initial Projection Sequence</u> (1970 to 1975)

3. The initial step entails cohort survival of the July 1, 1970 population matrix to July 1, 1975 by employing white/nonwhite, and male/female age-specific survival rates. For example, the cohort aged 0 to 4 years in 1970 will age to between 5 and 9 years by 1975; the procedures are defined by the following formulae:

$$_{5-9}P_{1975} = \left[_{0-4}S_{1970-1975} \right] \left[_{0-4}P_{1970} \right]$$

$$_{10-14}P_{1975} = \left[_{5-9}S_{1970-1975} \right] \left[_{5-9}P_{1970} \right]$$

$$\cdot$$
$$\cdot$$
$$\cdot$$

$$_{60-64}P_{1975} = \left[_{55-59}S_{1970-1975} \right] \left[_{55-59}P_{1970} \right]$$

$$_{65+}P_{1975} = \left[_{60-64}S_{1970-1975} \right] \left[_{60-64}P_{1970} \right] +$$

$$\left[_{65+}S_{1970-1975} \right] \left[_{65+}P_{1970} \right]$$

where the survival rate S is specific to the 1970 to 1975 period, and is unique to each male/female, white/nonwhite age sector. In effect, a set of 52 separate linear equations is established, each solved independently. The technique employed is presented in:

Donald A. Krueckeberg and Arthur L. Silvers,
Urban Planning Analysis: Methods and Models
(New York: Wiley, 1974).

The survival rates were secured from:

U.S. Bureau of the Census, Current Popula-
tion Reports, Series P-25, No. 704,
"Projections of the Population of the
United States: 1977 to 2050," U.S.
Government Printing Office, Washington,
D.C., 1977.

4. 1975 labor force participation rates are
applied to the survived populations aged 16
to 64 years to establish the labor force
supply that would evolve absent migration.
For each sex-color subpopulation, the following series of equations were carried out, with
10 years intervals employed between 24 and 64
years of age span.

$$16\text{-}19^{LFS}1975 = \left[16\text{-}19^{SP}1975\right]\left[16\text{-}19^{LFPR}1975\right]$$

$$20\text{-}24^{LFS}1975 \quad \left[20\text{-}24^{SP}1975\right]\left[20\text{-}24^{LFPR}1975\right]$$

$$\vdots$$

$$55\text{-}64^{LFS}1975 \quad \left[55\text{-}64^{SP}1975\right]\left[55\text{-}64^{LFPR}1975\right]$$

where: LFS_{1975} = the age-specific labor
                        force supply (1975)

SP_{1975} = age-specific survived
                        population

$LFPR_{1975}$ = age-specific labor force
                        participation rate

For subsequent iterations of the model (1975
to 1980 to 1985), the labor force participation rates are projected via 24 separate
linear equations (ten-year intervals for each
population subgroup), each solved independ-
endently, according to the methodology
specified in:

Bureau of Labor Statistics, <u>Monthly Labor Review</u>, December 1976, pp. 3-13.

The procedure is represented by the equation:

$$LFPR_{1980} = P + \left[C \times T \right] - \left[I \times D_2 \right]$$

where: P = 1975 labor force participation rate

C = average annual rate of change (from 1970 to 1975 least squares equation)

T = years into future (5)

I = formula for sum of integers between 1 and n (total projection time span), n(n+1)/2, to create an approximate exponential smooth path.

D_2 = C divided by total projection span n.

<u>Migration Determination</u> (1970 to 1975)

5. Labor force demand is a function of the 1975 employment levels within New York City (a function of the 1980 and 1985 employment projections for subsequent model iterations). Employment levels are translated to labor force implications by exogeneously specified (independently projected) commutation ratios (the ratio of jobs within the city to resident workforce), the extrapolation of historic relationships of the workplace location of resident work force, and unemployment rate assumptions. The final step in the labor force demand calculation is the equation:

$$LFD = \frac{REmp}{1 = UR}$$

where: LFD = labor force demand
REmp = resident employes
1 - UR = 1 - unemployment rate (the complement of the unemployment rate)

The unemployment rates for 1980 and 1985 were established via least squares extrapolations of historical unemployment rate data.

6. The differential between labor force supply and labor force demand establishes the base migration parameter. The latter is pyramided to total migration (for the population below 65 years of age) via the 1975 ratio of total survived population (below 65 years of age) to 1975 labor force demand.

7. Migration disaggregation (total migration assigned to the age cells - below 65 years of age - of the four population subgroups) is operationalized on the basis of the migrational pattern evidenced over the 1960 to 1970 intercensal period. This was secured from:

   Gladys K. Bowles, Calvin L. Beale, and Everett S. Lee, Net Migration of the Population, 1960-1970 by Age, Sex, and Color, Part I -- Northeastern States and Counties (Athens, Georgia: Economic Research Service, U. S. Department of Agriculture; The Institute for Behavioral Research, University of Georgia; Research Applied to National Needs, National Science Foundation, 1975).

   The general procedure for obtaining the 1960 to 1970 pattern was a residual technique, expressed algebraically for each age, sex, and color sector by:

   $$M_{1960-1970} = (P_{1970} - P_{1960}) - N_{1960-1970}$$

   The standardization of this historical matrix to the 1970 to 1975 total migration (under 65 years of age) is based upon an allocation ratio:

   $$R = \frac{M - TM}{AM}$$

   where: M = Total Net Migration (1970 to 1975) under 65 years of age
            TM = Total Historical Migration (1960 to 1970) under 65 years of age
            AM = Sum of the absolute values of Net Historical Migration (1950 to 1970) under 65 years of age

Each age cell is then adjusted individually according to its historical attributes - either positive or negative migration. For positive historical migration:

$$NM = (1 + R) \cdot HM$$

For negative historical migration:

$$NM = (1 - R) \cdot HM$$

where: NM = net migration (1970 to 1975) by cohort

HM = historical net migration (1960 to 1970) by cohort

8. Elderly migration rates (white, nonwhite; male, female) were calibrated on the basis of 1970 to 1975 Medicare enrollment data. The migration rate is defined as:

$$MR = \frac{NM_{65+}}{SP_{65+}} \quad \text{(65 years and over)}$$

where: NM_{65+} = net migration (1970 to 1975) 65 years of age and over

SP_{65+} = survived elderly population (from 1970 base)

The survived elderly population (SP) was determined by aging both the 1970 Medicare totals (by sex and color) via 1970 to 1975 survival rates and the 60-to 64-years-of-age groups of 1970. The residuals of the sums of the latter and the 1975 Medicare totals were assumed to represent the net elderly migration totals for the four population subgroups. The subsequent rate determinations were held constant for the succeeding iterations of the model (to 1980 and 1985, respectively).

9. The output of the preceding calculations was the 1970 to 1975 migration matrix comprising 52 cells directly corresponding to the format of the basic data input (step 1).

Final Population Levels (1975)

10. The migration matrix was added to the initial output (the 1970 population matrix aged to 1975) of the cohort survival analysis, yielding the final 1975 population estimates (or projections). For each age sector (excluding the under-5-years-of-age categories), the following equation details this procedure:

$$P_{1975} = SP_{1970-1975} + NM_{1970-1975}$$

where: SP = survived population by sector
        NM = net migration by sector

11. To determine the under-five-years-of-age sectors, cohort specific birth rates are applied to the final cohorts (established in step 10) of women of childbearing age (10 to 49 years of age). For example, the births produced by the 25-to 29-years-of-age female sector (either white or nonwhite), are calculated by:

$$_{0-4}P_{1975} = \left[_{25-29}B \right] \left[_{25-29}{}^{f}P_{1975} \right] \left[\begin{array}{c} p(m) \ or \\ p(f) \end{array} \right]$$

where: $_{25-29}B$ = birth rate specific to the 25-to 29-years-of-age group for the 1970 to 1975 period, adjusted by historic differentials between the crude birth rate of the city and nation

$_{25-29}{}^{f}P_{1975}$ = female population 25 to 29 years of age in 1975

p(m) or p(f)   = proportion of births male or female as determined by historical patterns (constant through all age sectors)

The final 1975 population (0 to 4 years of age) is determined by applying the average 1970 to 1975 survival rate specific to the 0-to 4-years-of-age sector of each of the four population subgroups, or:

$$\text{total 1975 } P_{0-4} = \left[1975^P 0_{-4} \right] \left[0_{-4}S_{1970-1975} \right]$$

The birth rates were secured from:

U.S. Bureau of the Census, Current Population Reports, Series P-25, No. 704, "Projections of the Population of the United States: 1977 to 2050," U. S. Government Printing Office, Washington, D.C., 1977.

12. The survived births (male, female, white, nonwhite) are summed with the corresponding migration totals for the 0-to 4-years-of-age categories, and entered into the final population matrix. This 52 cell matrix corresponds directly to the 1970 base equivalent and represents the 1975 population estimate (projection) for 1975.

Model Reiteration

13. The final 1975 population matrix serves as the population base for the 1975 to 1980 projection interval, with the preceding set of calculations repeated for this period, with the exceptions and modifications noted previously. The final output, the 1980 matrix, subsequently serves as the population base for the final projection interval (1980 to 1985) where the overall process is reiterated once again.

14. For each of the projection years, the population is converted to households. (The conversion routine is detailed after the employment projection model is reviewed).

THE ECONOMIC PROJECTION METHODOLOGY

Within the component model of population change,
the migration variable will increase in importance as
the size (in terms of population level and area) of the
geographic focus of application decreases. Its significance is further accentuated when the analysis
centers on individual population age cohorts. Unfortunately, the migrational component is the most difficult to project, primarily because of the lack of
short interval time series data accounts analogous to
those documenting natural increase (annual survival and
birth rates, for example). Consequently, to avoid
rigid, mechanical, and, most likely, inadequate extrapolations of past census data, interest has centered
on linking migration to independent projections of
employment.[6] The underlying rationale suggests that
movements of people (migration) are related to relative
economic opportunity - that the major determination of
migration is economic in nature. Although a myriad of
factors are operative, and the web of causal relationships very complex, the New York City model has premised migration as a function of projected employment.

As has been described in step 5 of the preceding
discussion (see also Exhibit 1), city employment levels
in 1975, 1980, and 1985 were converted to resident
workforce parameters, and subsequently, to labor force
demand. The gap between this demand function and labor
force supply - the latter established by a "closed" cohort survival analysis and projections of labor force
participation rates - was assumed to induce migration.
Consequently, a critical dimension of the overall model
is the employment projection routine, the outlines of
which are described in the following analysis.

The Models

Four different models have been employed to forecast employment growth in New York City via two 5-year
increments from 1975 to 1985. Three of the four are
predicated on, and constrained by, exogeneous national
projections, i.e., the patterns of growth and decline
in New York City are linked to (or are a function of)
the broader performance of the national economy. The
linkages are specified differently by each model,
although the step-down procedure is similar for all
three models. Initially, two alternative step-down
methods were tested. The first involved a two-step

process, with the Middle Atlantic Division (New York, New Jersey, and Pennsylvania) employed as an intermediary between New York City and the nation, i.e., the Middle Atlantic Division's employment was projected as a function of national change, with New York City's future employment subsequently cast as a function of the divisional projections. The second linked New York City directly to the national experience - directly stepped down from the exogeneous national projections. After close examination of the test results, which differed only marginally, it was decided to fully operationalize only the latter procedure.

The fourth model differs from the first three in that the projections for New York City are made independent of national or divisional activity. Therefore, it does not involve a step-down procedure. The use of these four models simultaneously, then, establishes a projection package which provides four independent sets of results, the resolution of which will be examined subsequently. First, however, a brief description of the individual models is warranted, with the equation subscripts and superscripts defined as follows:

E = employment level
i = industry group
m = time increment (5 year periods)
t = time period
n = nation
c = New York City
a = intercept of least squares equation
b = slope of least squares equation

Constant Share. The major premise of the constant share model is that the historic or current share of national employment secured by a subarea will persist (remain constant) over time. Applied to New York City's industrial sectors, this model will project their growth at the same rate as that of their national counterparts. The controlling factors in the model are the set of exogeneous national projections and the baseline ratio of city employment to national employment. Algebraically, these relationships are specified as:

$$E^{ic}_{1980} = \left[\frac{E^{ic}_{1975}}{D^{in}_{1975}} \right] E^{in}_{1980}$$

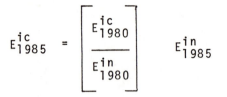

$$E_{1985}^{ic} = \left[\frac{E_{1980}^{ic}}{E_{1980}^{in}}\right] E_{1985}^{in}$$

Simple Shift-Share. The shift-share model as employed
here augments the constant-share procedure by delineating the shift which can occur over time in a subarea's
share of national employment. A shift component is
derived as a function of historically calibrated changes
in share which is subsequently used in the projection
routine to modify the constant share output. The
algebraic format is as follows:

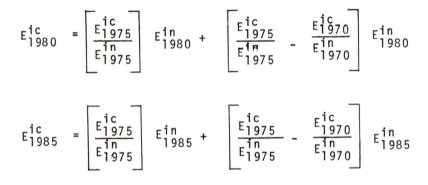

$$E_{1980}^{ic} = \left[\frac{E_{1975}^{ic}}{E_{1975}^{in}}\right] E_{1980}^{in} + \left[\frac{E_{1975}^{ic}}{E_{1975}^{in}} - \frac{E_{1970}^{ic}}{E_{1970}^{in}}\right] E_{1980}^{in}$$

$$E_{1985}^{ic} = \left[\frac{E_{1975}^{ic}}{E_{1975}^{in}}\right] E_{1985}^{in} + \left[\frac{E_{1975}^{ic}}{E_{1975}^{in}} - \frac{E_{1970}^{ic}}{E_{1970}^{in}}\right] E_{1985}^{in}$$

OBERS Shift-Share. This is a modified double exponential model with an implicit shift or "competitive
component" combining the step down parameter of the
constant-share model and the trend extrapolation feature of the simple regression model (the fourth model
which will be subsequently examined). The OBERS model
was developed by a research group from the Office of
Business Economics (now the Bureau of Economic Analysis)
and the Economic Research Service of the U. S. Department of Commerce, hence the acronym OBERS. The technique yields a trend extrapolation of an area's historic
percentage share of national employment for a given
industry. The procedures fits a least squares regression line to the logarithm of area percentage shares
against the logarithm of time. This is expressed
quantitatively via the following equations:

Using least squares linear regression:

$$\log\frac{E_t^{ic}}{E_t^{in}} = a + b^{ic}\log t \qquad t = 1 \text{ to } 6 \text{ (1970 to 1975)}$$

then

$$E_{1980}^{ic} = \left[\text{antilog}\left(\log\frac{E_{1975}^{ic}}{E_{1975}^{in}} + b^{ic}\log5\right) \right] E_{1980}^{in}$$

$$E_{1980}^{ic} = \left[\text{antilog}\left(\log\frac{E_{1975}^{ic}}{E_{1975}^{in}} + b^{ic}\log10\right) \right] E_{1985}^{in}$$

<u>Simple Regression</u>. The model comprises a single variable extrapolation regressing historical employment data against time. It is the only model of the four that does not involve a step down process, i.e., it is independent of national and/or regional activity. Consequently, the quantitative process - simple, least squares linear regression - defines the historical trendline in an area irrespective of events in larger arenas. It is algebraically defined as follows:

Using least squares linear regression:

$$E_t^{ic} = a + b^{ic}(t) \qquad t = 1 \text{ to } 6 \text{ (1970 to 1975)}$$

then,

$$E_{1980}^{ic} = E_{1975}^{ic} + b^{ic}(5)$$

$$E_{1985}^{ic} = E_{1975}^{ic} + b^{ic}(10)$$

The Data

The basic data set was drawn from the standardized
employment accounts of the Bureau of Labor Statistics.[7]
Included within this base is nonfarm wage and salary
and civilian government employment. It does not include
proprietors, the self-employed, unpaid volunteer or
family workers, farm workers, or domestic workers.
Since the national projection sets are defined in terms
of total employment, the preceding data had to be modified to include the self-employed and unpaid family
workers. Based on historical census data tabulations
disaggregating industrial sector employment by class of
worker, a series of multipliers were developed for each
industrial sector to convert the raw input data to a
total employment equivalent.

The following employment sector partitions were
used:

> Mining
> Construction
> Manufacturing
> Transportation and Public Utilities
> Wholesale and Retail Trade
> Finance, Insurance, and Real Estate
> Services
> Government

The National Projections

Through 1977, the actual employment experience of
New York City and the nation was available. For 1980
and 1985, the national projections of the Bureau of
Labor Statistics (U. S. Department of Labor) were
employed.[8] Since the national forecasts were predicated on a base year of full employment approximating
long-run potential (an optimistic scenario), two sets
of New York City projections were made. First, the
national forecasts were used directly (which served as
input into three of the four models). Second, to derive an alternative national base, the individual employment sectors (national) were scaled up or down,
based upon a set of scalers relating actual 1975 employment to projected 1975 employment. In total,
seven sets of New York City projections were carried
out.

The Presentation Procedure

The results of the individual employment projection models have been averaged to provide an overall measure of central tendency, which is termed the central projection. This was not a purely mechanical derivation, however. If an individual projection was so extreme as to be highly unlikely under any plausable future conditions, it was discarded. Consequently, the central projections for each industrial sector were calculated on different numbers of model inputs, expressed algebraically as:

$$_{cp}E_{1980}^{ic} \quad = \quad \frac{\Sigma E_{1980}^{ic}}{n} \quad = \quad \frac{\Sigma E_{1980}^{ic}}{n}$$

where: n = number of individual projections
        cp = central projection

The central projection served as the working parameter for the subsequent determination of labor force demand. However, for analytical purposes, the feasible range within which the projections could vary but still have as strong probability of occuring was delineated. A band of likelihood was derived (with no formal statistical meaning to this terminology), providing some measure of dispersion or variation about the central projection. The operational procedure was similar to that of a mean deviation, which provides a measure smaller in magnitude than that which would be obtained through a standard deviation. It is computationally expressed as:

$$\frac{\Sigma \left| _{cp}E_{1980}^{ic} - E_{1980}^{ic} \right|}{n}$$

When this quantity was added to and subtracted from the central projection, the high and low boundaries, respectively, were specified. This is a purely descriptive band to which no theoretical connotations should be attached. Consequently, the data is presented in the main body of the report in the following format:

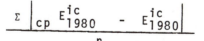

High	Central Projection	Low
$_{H}E_{1980}^{ic}$	$_{cp}E_{1980}^{ic}$	$_{L}E_{1980}^{ic}$

HOUSEHOLD GENERATION

The population projections for 1975, 1980, and 1985 were converted to the total number of households according to age of the household head. The methodological procedures comprised nine major computational steps.

Historical Data

1. For the United States and New York City, the number of households by the age of the head of household for 1970 was secured from the decennial census.

Age of Head	U.S.	N.Y.C.
24		
25-34		
35-44		
45-64		
65+		
Total		

2. The population for both areas was disaggregated into the same age partitions, and headship rates determined for each age category according to the formula:

$$\frac{25\text{-}34^{HH}1970}{25\text{-}34^{P}\ 1970} = 25\text{-}34^{HR}1970$$

where: HH = heads of household
          P = population
          HR = headship rate

3. The rate of change of the headship rate between 1960 and 1970 for both the nation and New York City calculated and the ratio between the two rates determined.

National Projections

4. The projected households by age of the head
   of household for the United States for 1975,
   1980, and 1985 were obtained. The corresponding population projections (by age) were
   used to establish age-specific headship rates,
   corresponding in format to steps 1 and 2
   above. The household projections were
   secured from:

   > U. S. Bureau of the Census, <u>Current Popu-
   > lation Reports</u>, Series P-25, No. 607
   > "Projections of the Number of Households
   > and Families: 1975 to 1990," U. S.
   > Government Printing Office, Washington,
   > D.C., 1975.

5. For each age-specific rate, the percentage
   change over the three five-year intervals was
   determined (1970 to 1975; 1975 to 1980; and
   1980 to 1985). For example, for the 25 to 34
   years of age category between 1975 and 1980,
   the rate of change is defined as:

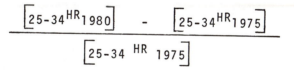

$$\frac{\left[25\text{-}34^{HR}1980\right] - \left[25\text{-}34^{HR}1975\right]}{\left[25\text{-}34 \ ^{HR} \ 1975\right]}$$

National-New York City Linkage

6. The national rates of change were modified
   (adjusted) by the historic national-New York
   City differential evidenced over the 1960 to
   1970 period (the ratios calculated in step 3).

7. The adjusted rates of change were applied to
   1970 New York City headship rates, deriving
   age-specific headship rates for 1975, 1980,
   and 1985.

New York City Households

8. The headship matrix (rate of age) for New
   York City for each projection date was applied
   to the corresponding population projection
   (total population by age) to establish the

total number of households by the age of head.
For example, in 1980, the algebraic procedure
is as follows:

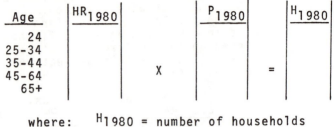

Age
24
25-34
35-44
45-64
65+

where: H_{1980} = number of households

P_{1980} = total population

HR_{1980} = headship rate

9. The final output was a matrix of the total
    number of households partitioned by the age
    of the household head:

Age	1970	1975	1980	1985
24				
25-34				
35-44				
45-64				
65+				

Household Configurations

10. Following the methodology depicted above, the
     specific household configurations were derived.
     The final output was a matrix of the total
     number of households categorized by household
     type.

Household Type	1970	1975	1980	1985
Primary Families				
Husband-Wife				
Male Head-No Wife Present				
Female Head-No Husband Present				

THE ASSUMPTIONS AND LIMITATIONS

The projections of this study must be viewed as forecasts unique to and dependent upon certain major assumptions. They represent a path of expectations which will be realized only to the extent that the hypothesized relationships of the model approximate future reality. Certainly, questions of likelihood and probability arise; we would be remiss if the limitations attendant to specific methodological operations were not made explicit. The list which follows isolates some of the more pivotal assumptions, as well as their possible consequences.

1. The linkage of migration solely to changing levels of employment may understate the scale of migration. As will be evident as the balance of the study is reviewed, New York City experienced substantial net outmigration over the 1960 to 1970 period, a time when the city's total employment held virtually constant. This incongruity was largely sustained by the changing proportion of in-city jobs held by commuters. (See paragraph 3 below.) This population overflow was spearheaded by white households in the process of childrearing; with the decline of fertility, however, this pattern may be of declining significance.

2. While total nonelderly migration in this model is dependent on employment change, its detailed allocation to age, sex, and color specified subpopulations is based on the historic intercensal (1960 to 1970) pattern, adjusted to the overall projected total. To the degree that the pattern has evolved, distortions are introduced into the migration matrices of each projection interval. Nevertheless, since there is little empirical evidence available to modify it, the pattern (but not magnitude) of migration is held constant through the projection time span.

3. In translating projected employment to labor force demand, the assumption was made that New York City residents would secure an increasing proportion of the city's jobs. To the degree that this premise is unwarranted, migration may again be understated.

4. Similarly, in translating workforce (total
    employed) to labor force implications, the
    projected unemployment rates for 1980 and
    1985 may be too high. If the rates were
    lowered, the labor force demand would be
    reduced, thereby stimulating outmigration.
    Consequently, in conjunction with the pre-
    ceding assumption, we may be underestimating
    the magnitude of outmigration.

5. The potential flow of illegal immigration and
    its unrecorded base within the city have not
    been taken into account, because of the lack
    of data describing the phenomenon.

    Certainly, other limitations are inherent to the
balance of the model's operations. Not least among
them is the issue of future government policies. In
any case, the main outlines and contours of the process
of change are probably captured by the framework we
have devised. The pattern of the results is probably
on target; their size and scale are subject to more
uncertainty. Thus, the projections presented here
are far from definitive. Rather, they represent a
best estimate based on reasonable methodologies within
the state of the art.

Notes

1. For example, see: Henry S. Shryock, Jacob S. Siegal, and Associates, The Methods and Materials of Demography (U.S. Bureau of the Census, U. S. Government Printing Office, Washington, D.C., 1975).

2. Ira S. Lowry, Migration and Metropolitan Growth: Two Analytical Models (San Francisco, California: Chandler, 1966), pp. 40-44.

3. Similar approaches are reported in: Pennsylvania Governor's Office of State Planning and Development Pennsylvania Projection Series: Population and Labor Force, Report No. 73 (Harrisburg, Pa.: Commonwealth of Pennsylvania, 1973); Joe W. Lee and William B. D. Hong, "Regional Demographic Projections: 1960-1985," 1972 Regional Economic Projection Series, Report No. 72-R-1 (Washington, D.C.: National Planning Association, 1972).

4. Donald A. Krueckeberg and Arthus L. Silvers, Urban Planning Analysis: Methods and Models (New York: Wiley, 1974), p. 276.

5. Richard Irwin, Guide for Local Area Projections, U. S. Bureau of the Census Technical Paper No. 39, U.S. Government Printing Office, Washington, D.C.,1977, p.16.

6. For example, see discussions in: Donald B. Pittinger, Projecting State and Local Populations (Cambridge, Massachusetts, 1976), Chapter 8.

7. U. S. Department of Labor, Bureau of Labor Statistics, Employment and Earnings, U. S. Government Printing Office, Washington, D.C., monthly.

8. Bureau of Labor Statistics, U.S. Department of Labor, The Structure of the U.S. Economy in 1980 and 1985, Bulletin 1831 (Washington, D.C.: Government Printing Office, 1975); Howard Friedenberg and Robert Bretzfelder, "Tracking and BEA State Economic Projections," Survey of Current Business, Vol. 56, No. 4 (April 1976), pp. 22-29.

Chapter 2

THE EMPLOYMENT CONTEXT: NATIONAL AND REGIONAL

INTRODUCTION

All too often we bask in the comfortable but unsub-
stantiated assumption that New York is unique and that
its destiny is its own resolve. However, whatever
their virtues or demerits, these notions are of limited
viability. New York City does not function within a
vacuum but is enmeshed in a dynamic of much broader
scope and origin, one whose reverberations penetrate
each and every one of the city's social and economic
parameters. Unfortunately, the immediacies of appar-
ently local problems often tend to obscure the fact
that these problems are intimately tied to broader
shifts taking place in the locus of economic and demographic development within the nation as a whole.

Nor is the city unique; its fate is shared by a
host of other similarly positioned jurisdictions. Consequently, the interpretation of New York's economic
past and future requires a frame of reference beyond
that of the city's unique particulars. As a prelude
to examining the historic and projected changes in
New York City employment, then, it is useful to define
the broader context within which they take place as
well as the appropriate "backdrop" for their analysis.

Obsolete reference frameworks are an ever present
peril; so, too, are hastily adopted new conventions if
they serve to reflect only momentary aberrants. Yet,
the regional analytical perspective is proving to be
of long-term duration. The time-cycle between nascent
recognition and conventional wisdom has transpired in
rapid fashion. Indeed, the "rise of the Sunbelt" and

the "decline of the Northeast" are terms of such current prominence that it is difficult to recall a time
without them. However, they encompass events which are
not new but represent the accelerated evolution of
established trendlines. *A very powerful momentum has
built up over the past fifteen years, sweeping employment and population growth away from the older metropolitan centers of the Northeast and North Central
states to the newer growth poles of the South and West.*

In the past decade, when this new dynamic was
emerging, the major political convulsions and confronta-
tions centered on the internal shifts taking place within metropolitan areas. Riveting our attentions and
energies were the tensions between the traumas of the
central city and the growth - aspirations of suburbia.
Unnoticed was the fact that the industrial belt from
Boston to St. Louis, which Wilbur Thompson calls the
"American Ruhr," was beginning a long-term downward
slide.[1] Only when the underlying forces reached critical mass, and momentum snowballed, was their significance fully appreciated. When events reach this
stage, the contours of change become etched so deeply
that the opportunities for their deflection are minimal without drastic restructuring. *The analogy between
the decline of the aging northern industrial crescent
and the long-term transformation of our older central
cities is increasingly - and uncomfortably - apt.*

The tabular presentations that immediately follow
serve to define and document the regional perspective.
The economic and social indicators have been partitioned into two broad categories, economic shifts and
population flows. The organizational format is predicated on providing a broad overview of total employment change before isolating its specific subsectors,
the first of which is manufacturing, historically construed as basic or not population-dependent. Several
dimensions of population shifts are then considered,
followed by two additional employment clusters which
are assumed, realizing some degree of distortion in
this assumption, to be nonbasic or population-dependent, private nonmanufacturing and government. Briefly,
the analytical subsets are linked by the following
equation:

        Total Employment = Manufacturing + Private
                            Nonmanufacturing + Government

TOTAL EMPLOYMENT SHIFTS

What are the long-term patterns of employment
change? Assembled in Exhibit 1 are the overall national
employment totals for 1960 and 1975 disaggregated on a
region and division basis. In this fifteen-year period,
the employment base of the United States has increased
by 46.6 percent or by 23.9 million jobs. This growth
was far from evenly distributed throughout the country,
however. While the Northeast secured only a 21.7 percent increase and the North Central Region 36.2 percent,
rates of growth far below the national average, employment in the South and West expanded by nearly 70 percent.
Indeed though the South's total employment in 1960, 13.8
million, was substantially below that of the Northeast's
15.2 million and the North Central Region's 15.3 million,
by 1975 it has evolved into the dominant employment
locus of the country, encompassing 23.4 million jobs.
Thus, in fifteen years, the South outdistanced both the
Northeast and North Central Regions, which hover slightly
below and above the 20 million job mark, respectively.

When the focus is narrowed to the divisional partitions, the relative stagnation of the older industrial
heartland is further highlighted. *The most laggard part
of the United States is the Middle Atlantic Division,
comprising New York, New Jersey, and Pennsylvania.* Here
employment increased by less than two additional jobs
for every ten existing in 1960. Even New England, whose
long historic decline in relative position has been often
observed, fared better, adding three jobs for every ten
that existed in 1960. The East North Central Division's
performance replicates that of New England, i.e., three
additional jobs for every ten existing in 1960. The
West North Central Division, on the other hand, added
five jobs for every ten that preexisted. Even this last
pattern stands in marked contrast to the divisional
equivalents in the South and West, where even the weakest division shows growth on the order of seven additional jobs for every ten that existed in 1960.

Within this fifteen-year span there are compelling
patterns of variation that speak to the near-term
future. Exhibit 2 details the regional shares of the
nation's total growth for the three five-year periods
between 1960 and 1975. The weakness of the Northeast
and the growing strength of the South were clear from
1960 to 1965, a period of only modest national performance. The former accounted for only 14.5 percent of
the United States employment gains, while the latter
garnered 38.5 percent. The boom period of 1965 to 1970

EXHIBIT 2-1
TOTAL EMPLOYMENT CHANGE: 1960-1975[1]
BY REGION AND DIVISION
(Numbers in thousands)

Region and Division	1960	1975	Change: 1960 to 1975 Number	Percent
Northeast Region	*15,119.5*	*18,535.4*	*3,305.9*	*21.7*
Middle Atlantic Division	11,676.4	13,864.9	2,188.5	18.7
New England Division	3,553.1	4,670.5	1,117.4	31.4
North Central Region	*15,291.8*	*20,826.7*	*5,534.9*	*36.2*
East North Central Division	11,318.1	14,957.5	3,639.4	32.2
West North Central Division	3,973.7	5,869.2	1,895.5	47.7
South Region	*13,818.0*	*23,480.3*	*9,662.3*	*69.9*
South Atlantic Division	7,054.2	12,078.8	5,024.6	71.2
East South Central Division	2,606.0	4,353.0	1,747.0	67.0
West South Central Division	4,157.8	7,048.5	2,890.7	69.5
West Region	*7,734.3*	*13,110.4*	*5,376.1*	*69.5*
Mountain Division	1,765.9	3,353.9	1,588.0	89.9
Pacific Division	5,968.4	9,756.5	3,788.1	63.5
U. S. TOTAL[2]	52,073.6	75,952.8	23,879.2	46.6

Notes; 1. Employees on nonagriculture payrolls as of March of the respective years.
2. Excludes Hawaii and Alaska

Source: U.S. Department of Labor, Bureau of Labor Statistics, <u>Employment and Earnings</u>, Washington, D.C.: U.S. Government Pringint Of ice, monthly.

EXHIBIT 2-2
REGIONAL GROWTH SHARES OF
TOTAL EMPLOYMENT CHANGE: 1960-1975[1]
(Numbers in thousands)

Region	Absolute Growth Increment			Percentage Share of National Growth		
	1960-1965	1965-1970	1970-1975	1960-1965	1965-1970	1970-1975
United States Total[2]	6,041.9	11,911.4	5,925.9	100.0	100.0	100.0
Northeast Region	875.7	2,465.9	-35.7	14.5	20.7	-0.6
Middle Atlantic Division	594.2	1,818.2	-223.9	9.8	15.3	-3.8
New England Division	281.5	647.7	188.2	4.7	5.4	3.2
North Central Region	1,422.2	3,240.6	872.1	23.6	27.2	14.7
East South Central Division	989.7	2,332.6	317.6	16.4	19.6	5.4
West North Central Division	432.5	908.5	554.5	7.2	7.6	9.4
South Region	2,323.6	4,033.6	3,305.1	38.5	33.9	55.8
South Atlantic Division	1,182.8	2,146.6	1,695.2	19.6	18.0	28.6
East South Central Division	509.4	668.5	569.1	8.4	5.6	9.6
West South Central Division	631.4	1,218.5	1,040.8	10.5	10.2	17.6
West Region	1,420.4	2,171.3	1,784.4	23.5	18.2	30.1
Mountain Division	322.8	493.7	771.5	5.3	4.1	13.0
Pacific Division	1,097.6	1,677.6	1,012.9	18.2	14.1	17.1

Notes:
1. Employees on nonagriculture payrolls as of March of the respective periods.
2. Excludes Hawaii and Alaska.
3. Numbers and percents may not add due to rounding.

Source: U.S. Department of Labor, Bureau of Labor Statistics, Employment and Earnings, Washington, D.C.: U. S. Government Printing Office, monthly.

obscured this differential, dampening the interregional spread. Yet, even under what now appears to have been an exceptional growth period in American history, the South encompassed 33.9 percent of the national expansion, and the Northeast only 20.7 percent.

The slowdown in the pace of growth of the overall economy from 1970 to 1975 spawned a unique absolute job decline in the Northeast, with more than 35,000 jobs lost. The South, conversely, gained more than 3.3 million jobs, an addition that represents more than half of all the new economic growth in the United States from 1970 to 1975.

Within the Northeast, the variation between the Middle Atlantic and New England Divisions is most striking. In the first ten years of the period, it is the former that maintained the Northeast's vitality, with shares of national growth double and triple that of New England. From 1970 to 1975, however, the situation changes quite markedly. While the Middle Atlantic states lost 224,000 jobs, New England concurrently gained 188,000. Clearly, New England may have been an early loser, but its decline is bottoming out and it now appears to be stabilizing into slow but steady growth for the future. Nevertheless, it trails all the divisions save for the Middle Atlantic.

Is this a reflection of the Northeast becoming the focus of marginal employment opportunities? Does it imply that this region requires very substantial national growth before its resources are brought into the main stream? And, conversely, will it continue to lose out to more efficient and/or more desirable areas as soon as there is curtailment in the absolute levels of employment demand? In order to clarify these questions, further analysis of the underlying economic sectors is required. First, however, it may be useful to examine more closely the leading edge of decline in the Northeast - the Middle Atlantic Division.

The Middle Atlantic Division

In Exhibit 3 we have detailed the employment shifts for the states comprising this division (New York, New Jersey, and Pennsylvania), as well as for New York City, Philadelphia, and the balance of their respective states. The period 1960 to 1965 heralded the shifts that were to take place ten years later, with New York City losing jobs as the division in

EXHIBIT 2-3
TOTAL EMPLOYMENT CHANGE: MIDDLE ATLANTIC DIVISION: 1960-1975[1]
(Numbers in thousands)

Division and State	1960	1965	Change 1960-1965 Number	Change 1960-1965 Percent	Year 1970	Change 1965-1970 Number	Change 1965-1970 Percent	1975	Change 1970-1975 Number	Change 1970-1975 Percent
Middle Atlantic Division	11,676.4	12,270.6	594.2	5.1	14,088.8	1,818.2	13.8	13,864.9	-223.9	-1.6
New York State	6,102.1	6,333.5	231.4	3.8	7,159.1	825.6	13.0	6,881.5	-177.6	-3.9
New York City	3,557.7	3,554.0	-3.7	-0.1	3,817.2	263.2	7.4	3,378.7	-438.5	-11.5
Balance of State	2,544.4	2,779.5	235.1	9.2	3,341.9	562.4	20.2	3,502.8	160.9	4.8
New Jersey State	1,943.0	2,163.0	220.0	11.2	2,580.6	417.6	16.0	2,637.6	57.0	2.2
Pennsylvania State	3,631.3	3,774.1	142.8	3.9	4,349.1	575.0	15.2	4,345.8	-3.3	-0.1
Philadelphia City[2]	N.A.	N.A.	N.A.	N.A.	919.4	N.A.	N.A.	810.6	-108.8	-11.8
Balance of State	N.A.	N.A.	N.A.	N.A.	3,429.7	N.A.	N.A.	3,535.2	105.5	3.1

Notes: 1. Employees on nonagriculture payrolls as of March of the respective periods.
2. The data for Philadelphia City not available for 1960 and 1965. Additionally, the Philadelphia City totals are annual averages.

Source: U.S. Department of Labor, Bureau of Labor Statistics, Employment and Earnings, Washington, D.C.: U.S. Government Printing Office, monthly.

total added nearly 600,000 employees. If we consider
New York State sans New York City, it fared almost as
well as New Jersey. Bolstered by the suburbanization
of New York City and Philadelphia deeper into its
territories, New Jersey's 11.3 percent increase in employment dominated the positive side of the ledger.

The period from 1965 to 1970, one of enormous
economic vigor for the country as a whole, raised the
level of employment growth throughout the division, with
the earlier intradivisional balances being preserved.
From 1970 to 1975, however, the situation changes very
drastically - the division as a whole lost 224,000 jobs.
However, it is extremely important to note that the decline of both New York City (439,000 jobs) and Philadelphia (109,000 jobs) completely obscures the positive
growth of the balance of the division. Excluding these
two decline sectors, the Middle Atlantic states enjoyed
an increase in employment of 324,000 jobs. *This would
appear to indicate, then, that areas of stability and
vigor coexist in the presence of severe pockets of decline, raising a basic question: is the Northeast
problem one of massed concentrations of obsolete industrial cities, exerting a powerful influence throughout
the region? Or has a weakened regional structure
exacerbated the difficulties of the region's cities?
While the causal web may never be untangled, the con-
gruity of their plights is given emphasis by the virtual
identity of New York City's and Philadelphia's rate of
decline - 11.5 and 11.8 percent, respectively.*

MANUFACTURING EMPLOYMENT

Viewing employment in the aggregate tends to obscure the varying performances of major industrial subsectors. In this context, it appears that a major
swing element has been the change in manufacturing employment.

Manufacturing employment in the United States, as
shown in Exhibit 4, has shown minimal growth in the
fifteen years between 1960 to 1975 - increasing by
fewer than 1.5 million jobs or 8.8 percent. This pattern may not be unique to the United States but rather
is representative of the evolution that takes place
within an advanced technological society. The linkage
of productivity increases (generated by new approaches
to job rationalization and increased capital investment)
with the export of labor intensive manufacturing activity to foreign lower cost areas, imposes effective

EXHIBIT 2-4
MANUFACTURING EMPLOYMENT CHANGE: 1960-1975[1]
BY REGION AND DIVISION
(Numbers in thousands)

Region and Division	Year		Change 1960-1975	
	1960	*1975*	*Number*	*Percent*
Northeast Region	*5,620.6*	*4,839.2*	*-781.4*	*-13.9*
Middle Atlantic Division	4,172.8	3,547.1	-625.7	-15.0
New England Division	1,447.8	1,292.1	-155.7	-10.8
North Central Region	*5,579.9*	*5,814.3*	*234.4*	*4.2*
East North Central Division	4,586.4	4,577.8	-8.6	-0.2
West North Central Division	993.5	1,236.5	243.0	24.5
South Region	*3,650.5*	*5,146.5*	*1,496.0*	*41.0*
South Atlantic Division	2,013.1	2,614.2	601.1	29.9
East South Central Division	823.2	1,245.0	421.8	51.2
West South Central Division	814.2	1,287.3	473.1	58.1
West Region	*1,874.6*	*2,394.9*	*520.3*	*27.8*
Mountain Division	248.9	411.2	162.3	65.2
Pacific Division	1,625.7	1,983.7	358.0	22.0
U. S. TOTAL[2]	16,725.6	18,194.9	1,469.3	8.8

Notes: 1. Employees on nonagriculture payrolls as of March of the respective years.
2. Excludes Hawaii and Alaska

Source: U.S. Department of Labor, Bureau of Labor Statistics, Employment and Earnings, Washington, D.C.: U.S. Government Printing Office, monthly.

EXHIBIT 2-5
REGIONAL GROWTH SHARES OF MANUFACTURING EMPLOYMENT CHANGE: 1960-1975[1]
(Numbers in thousands)

Region	Absolute Growth Increment			Percentage Share of National Growth		
	1960-1965	1965-1970	1970-1975	1960-1965	1965-1970	1970-1975
United States Total[2]	722.9	2,213.4	-1,467.0	100.0	100.0	-100.0
Northeast Region						
Middle Atlantic Division	-89.4	187.8	-724.1	-12.4	8.5	-49.4
New England Division	29.7	77.1	-212.1	-2.8	3.5	-14.4
North Central Region						
East South Central Division	148.0	428.0	-585.4	20.5	19.3	-39.9
West North Central Division	41.7	195.7	5.6	5.8	8.8	0.4
South Region						
South Atlantic Division	250.4	424.3	-73.6	34.6	19.2	-5.0
East South Central Division	157.1	233.3	31.4	21.7	10.5	2.1
West South Central Division	113.1	293.9	66.1	15.6	13.3	4.5
West						
Mountain Division	25.4	82.9	54.0	3.5	3.7	3.7
Pacific Division	97.3	289.6	-28.9	13.5	13.1	-2.0

Notes: 1. Employees on nonagriculture payrolls as of March of the respective periods.
2. Excludes Hawaii and Alaska.
3. Numbers and percents may not add due to rounding.

Source: U.S. Edpartment of Labor, Bureau of Labor Statistics, <u>Employment and Earnings</u>, Washington, D.C.: U.S. Government Printing Office, monthly.

limits on employment growth. But within this relatively static national picture, the shifts between regions have been monumental. *The Northeast has lost over
781,000 manufacturing jobs from 1960 to 1975, 13.9 percent of its 1960 total.* The North Central Region experienced only minimal change, but the South increased
with enormous vigor, adding almost 1.5 million manufacturing jobs to its employment rolls. *Indeed the South,
in and of itself, fully accounted for the total U. S.
growth increment; the losses of the Northeast offset
the relatively small growth totals of the North Central
and West Regions.*

In 1960 the Northeast was the dominant manufacturing center of the nation, as evidenced by its 5.6
million job total. The North Central Region was closely
competitive, with employment at the 5.5 million level,
while the South had only 3.6 million manufacturing jobs.
By 1975, however, the South surpassed the Northeast and
now challenges the stagnant North Central Region. *But
it is the Middle Atlantic Division of the Northeast that
leads this sad procession of manufacturing employment
losers with a net decline of 625,000 jobs by 1975 -
fully 15 percent of its 1960 total.*

Again, the long-term trends mask periodic variation of vital import in viewing the short-term future.
The shifting patterns of growth are highlighted in
Exhibit 5, which delineates the regional growth shares
of manufacturing employment change by five-year intervals from 1960 through 1975. From 1960 to 1965, when
the absolute growth in manufacturing employment
nationally had slowed substantially, the Northeast lost
110,000 jobs. At the same time, the South secured the
bulk - 72 percent - of the national increase of 723,000
jobs. From 1965 to 1970, when the absolute national
growth increment tripled, the Northeast benefitted substantially, securing more than 264,000 jobs. The South,
however, was concurrently accumulating a higher and
higher level of critical mass, with a net growth of
951,000 jobs.

The broader dynamics change quite drastically from
1970 to 1975 when the nation as a whole lost nearly 1.5
million manufacturing jobs. *Almost 64 percent, more
than 936,000 jobs, were lost in the Northeast, a decline that represents the acceleration of the pattern
established in the 1960 to 1965 period.* The North
Central Region showed a major break in trend, losing
more than 500,000 jobs. The South and the West, conversely, struggled through this period of national
stress with small but significant gains.

The pattern that in the late 1920s <u>The Regional Plan of New York and Its Environs</u> anticipated for New York City (later confirmed, in the late 1950s, by Hoover and Vernon's key analysis for the New York Metropolitan Region Study) of a declining manufacturing base within New York City now seems to have spread to the entire region that dominates the older urban scene of America - the Northeast.[2] Increasingly enveloped within this transformation is the less senior but still aging industrial heartland of the United States, the North Central states. *Events once endemic to the metropolitan level - in particular employment decentralization - appear to have been amplified to new spatial scales and are now working themselves out over the entire geography of the country.*

<u>The Middle Atlantic Division</u>. Exhibit 6 details, by five-year periods, the major subareas of the Middle Atlantic Division. It is strikingly evident that the decline in manufacturing employment during the first ten years of the period under consideration was solely the province of New York City. Presently (1970 to 1975) it is a dominant theme throughout all division subareas. Every state, including the balance of New York and Pennsylvania, i.e., excluding New York City and Philadelphia, respectively, show absolute declines in manufacturing employment. However, more than 316,000 of the net loss of 724,000 manufacturing jobs in the Middle Atlantic Division accrued to these two cities. Each, remarkably, lost approximately 30 percent of its manufacturing employment over the five-year span. The losses of the balance of the division hovered around the 10 percent level.

The question to be raised, therefore, concerns the degree to which the overall northeastern experience is a function of the "writing off" of obsolete industrial infrastructures from the inventory of operational, and competitive, means of production, analogous to the scrapping of New England's mills several generations past. Certainly, the landscapes of New York City and Philadelphia, and the urban subcenters of their immediate hinterlands, are dominated by aging multifloored industrial structures, tied into the nineteenth century rail network. Their scale of vacancies is increasingly ominous with local jurisdiction struggling to uncover economically meaningful recycling formats.

EXHIBIT 2-6
MANUFACTURING EMPLOYMENT CHANGE[1]
MIDDLE ATLANTIC DIVISION: 1960-1975
(Numbers in thousands)

Division and State	1960	1965	Change 1960-1965 Number	Percent	1970	Change 1965-1970 Number	Percent	1975	Change 1970-1975 Number	Percent
Middle Atlantic Division	4,172.8	4,083.4	-89.4	-2.1	4,271.2	187.8	4.6	3,547.1	-724.1	-17.0
New York State	1,927.9	1,810.0	-117.9	-6.1	1,838.5	18.4	1.6	1,462.4	-376.1	-10.4
New York City	988.7	866.2	-122.5	-12.3	816.9	-39.2	-5.7	572.6	-244.3	-19.9
Balance of State	939.2	943.8	4.6	0.4	1,021.6	77.8	8.2	889.8	-131.8	-12.9
New Jersey State	794.6	807.9	14.4	1.7	884.2	76.2	9.4	735.3	-148.9	-16.8
Pennsylvania State	1,450.3	1,465.5	15.2	1.0	1,548.5	82.0	5.7	1,349.4	-199.1	-12.9
Philadelphia City[2]	N.A.	N.A.	N.A.	N.A.	237.8	N.A.	N.A.	165.5	-72.3	-20.3
Balance of State	N.A.	N.A.	N.A.	N.A.	1,310.7	N.A.	N.A.	1,183.9	-126.8	-9.7

Notes: 1. Employees on nonagriculture payrolls as of March of the respective periods.
2. The data for Philadelphia City not available for 1960 and 1965. Additionally, The Philadelphia City totals are annual averages.

Source: U.S. Department of Labor, Bureau of Labor Statistics, Employment and Earnings, Washington, D.C.: U.S. Government Printing Office, monthly.

The Role of Manufacturing

It has become *au courant* in recent years to stress
our societal transformation to a post-industrial format,
one in which nonmanufacturing employment, rather than
being merely a derivative of primary activity (manufacturing), manifests a life-force of its own. While
there is much substance in such generalizations, the
casual refutation of older reference frameworks may be
dangerous. A significant linkage persists between
manufacturing employment - and the wealth generated by
it - and both producer- and consumer-oriented service
industries, which, in whole or in part, serve to absorb
and multiply this largesse. The precise impact coefficients - the time lag between primary shrinkage and
secondary effect - is as yet obscure. It is further
complicated by great shifts in transfer payments in the
United States, which may mask the underlying process.
Nonetheless, as the patterns of change in nonmanufacturing employment are examined, this linkage should be
kept in mind.

But are trends destiny? Certainly the answer to
that question cannot be ascertained simply from the
'employment indicators presented so far. One critical
input into any economic future is the level of investment in new capital plant and infrastructure and the
regional allocation of that investment. In general,
new capital facilities are those that will ultimately
be utilized in preference to the old. The vital question concerns where they are being placed.

NONRESIDENTIAL CONSTRUCTION

Exhibit 7 summarizes the valuation of total private, nonresidential construction authorized from 1967
through the first five months of 1976. Under this
rubric is grouped all of the nation's activity in
creating the physical places where economic activity
is conducted. The pattern is an ominous one from the
point of view of the older northern regions. The
share of nonresidential investment developed in the
Northeast shrank consistently through the period under consideration, from a 21.7 percent annual average
from 1967 through 1969 to 15.9 percent annual average
from 1973 to 1975, and to a far from definitive but
forebodingly low 11.4 percent in the first five months
of 1976! The North Central Region conversely, held
relatively constant throughout these periods, generally
capturing about 25 percent of the national investment.

EXHIBIT 2-7
VALUATION OF TOTAL PRIVATE NONRESIDENTIAL
CONSTRUCTION AUTHORIZED 1967-1976
(Millions of Dollars; Numbers Represent
Annual Averages for the Periods Indicated)

Period	U. S. Total	Northeast Region	Annual Average Valuation North Central Region	South Region	West Region
1967-1969	11,683.3	2,540.7	3,119.8	3,395.8	2,627.0
1970-1972	14,277.5	2,641.1	3,409.5	4,734.4	3,492.5
1973-1975	17,932.1	2,848.4	4,431.2	6,157.5	4,495.0
1976[1]	6,420.6	728.9	1,601.1	2,295.8	1,794.8

Percent Distribution

Period	U. S. Total	Northeast Region	North Central Region	South Region	West Region
1967-1969	100.0	21.7	26.7	29.1	22.5
1970-1972	100.0	18.5	23.9	33.21	24.5
1973-1975	100.0	15.9	24.7	34.3	25.1
1976[1]	100.0	11.4	24.9	35.8	28.0

Note: 1. First five months, preliminary.

Source: U.S. Bureau of the Census, Construction Reports Series C20, U.S. Government Printing Office, Washington, D.C., monthly.

Once again it is the South and West that increasingly procure the bulk of new development, with the former enlarging its share from 29.1 percent to 35.8 percent from 1967 to 1976. The West's pattern of invigoration correlates significantly with that of the South; it is adding to and replenishing its nonresidential base accounting for 28.0 percent of current national totals, more than twice the magnitude of the Northeast. Significantly, the West was at parity with the latter area only eight years previously.

POPULATION FLOWS

Within the continental United States, it is the shift of population that serves both as signal and as instigator of economic growth and decline particularly in regard to nonmanufacturing activities. The new shopping center, in the absence of net new additional consumers to be serviced, can only flourish at the cost of the contraction of the old. The new field sales office, the growth of financial institutions, and the development of an interwoven set of service industries geared to local consumers, are all directly linked to this key variable.

The secular pattern of shift in the United States, as exemplified by westward movement, though perhaps as old as our history, has now been suddenly accentuated. Exhibit 8 tabulates the basic regional population changes that have occurred from 1960 to 1975. Of overriding consideration in viewing these regional performances is the *deceleration of national growth* -- from 18.5 percent from 1950 to 1960, to 13.4 percent from 1960 to 1970, and to 4.8 percent (which translates to an equivalent decade rate of 9.8 percent) from 1970 to 1975. For the entire 1960 to 1975 period, when the nation's population expanded by 18.8 percent, the Northeast and North Central States grew by only 10.7 and 11.7 percent, respectively. It was the South and West which gained by far the bulk of the population increases, as evidenced by growth rates of 23.9 and 35.0 percent, respectively. Indeed, in 1960 the West had only 60 percent of the population of the Northeast; by 1975, it broached the 75 percent mark. The South's 1960 population exceeded by ten million that of the Northeast; by 1975 this gap had nearly doubled.

The significance of these variations is given further emphasis in Exhibit 9, which brings the data through 1976 while also displaying the divisional

EXHIBIT 2-8
REGIONAL POPULATION CHANGE: 1960 TO 1975
(Numbers in thousands)

| Region | Population Totals | | | Period | | | | | |
| | 1960[1] | 1970[2] | 1975[3] | Numerical Change | | | Percentage Change | | |
				1960-1975	1960-1970	1970-1975	1960-1975	1960-1970	1970-1975
Northeast	44,678	49,061	49,461	4,783	4,383	400	10.7	9.8	0.8
North Central	51,619	56,593	57,669	6,050	4,974	1,076	11.7	9.6	1.9
South	54,973	62,812	68,112	13,140	7,839	5,300	23.9	14.3	8.4
West	28,053	34,838	37,878	9,825	6,785	3,040	35.0	24.2	8.7
U.S. TOTAL	179,323	203,304	213,120	33,797	23,981	9,816	18.8	13.4	4.8

1. April 1, 1960 census.
2. April 1, 1970 census as reported in source below.
3. July 1, 1975 provisional estimate.
4. Numbers may not add due to rounding.

U.S. Bureau of the Census, *Current Population Reports*, Series P-25, No. 640, "Estimates of the Population of States with Components of Change: 1970 to 1975," U.S. Government Printing Office, Washington, D.C., 1976.

EXHIBIT 2-9

REGIONAL POPULATION GROWTH PATTERNS: 1970 TO 1976

(Numbers in thousands)

Region and Division	1970[1]	1976[2]	Change 1970-1976 Number	Percent
NORTHEAST REGION				
New England	49,061	49,503	442	0.9
Middle Atlantic	11,847	12,221	374	3.2
	37,213	37,282	69	0.2
NORTH CENTRAL REGION				
East North Central	56,593	57,739	1,146	2.0
West North Central	40,266	40,934	668	1.7
	16,328	16,805	477	2.9
SOUTH REGION				
South Atlantic	62,812	68,855	6,043	9.6
East South Central	30,679	33,990	3,311	10.8
West South Central	12,808	13,661	853	6.7
	19,325	21,204	1,879	9.7
WEST REGION				
Mountain	34,838	38,562	3,724	10.7
Pacific	8,290	9,833	1,543	18.6
	26,549	28,729	2,180	8.2
U.S. TOTAL	203,304	214,659	11,355	5.6

Notes: 1. April 1, 1970 Census as reported in first source below.
2. July 1, 1976 estimate.

Source: U.S. Bureau of the Census, Current Population Reports, Series P-25, No. 640, "Estimates of the Population of States with Components of Change: 1970 to 1975," U.S. Government Printing Office, Washington, D.C., November 1976.

U.S. Bureau of the Census, Current Population Reports, Series P-20, No. 307, "Population Profile of the United States: 1976," U.S. Government Printing Office, Washington, D.C. April 1977.

experiences. New York City's immediate environment - the Middle Atlantic Division - shows the least growth of any divisional partition with a total population increase of only 69,000 people (0.2 percent) over the 1970 to 1976 period. The stagnation, as will be seen subsequently, is correlated with and underpins the performance of the nonmanufacturing employment sector.

Total population change, however, is the product of both net natural increases (births minus deaths) and net migration. Given the overall decline in the nation's birth rate, the latter assumes increased significance. Migration is a telling criterion of location shift by choice, of people seeking out "better" places to live. Whether because of climate, jobs, sheer restlessness, or whatever, migration data tend to gauge the locational preferences of Americans. In Exhibit 10 these are clearly defined. *The period from 1960 to 1970 appears to mark the terminal shift of population as a function of the agricultural revolution.* The West North Central Division, the bread basket of America, lost nearly 600,000 people through net migration during this period. Replicating this pattern was the East South Central Division; the dissolution of labor-intensive farming resulted in a net outmigration of nearly 700,000 people.

Concurrently, the West Region was the goal of the bulk of the movers, with the Pacific Division alone gaining more than 2.5 million individuals. Its lure was paralleled by the South Atlantic Division, with the great boom of Florida the leading attraction; this total division gained more than 1.3 million individuals. The Northeast, in part because of overseas inmigration, enjoyed a net addition of 375,000 individuals, the bulk of them concentrated in the New England Division.

The dynamic changes that have occurred since 1970 are of enormous significance to the pressures on land use as they relate to the economic adjustments taking place in the nation. The aging industrial belt is increasingly being vacated as a matter of conscious choice. *The North Central Region's 1970 and 1975 net outmigration, for example, approached the 900,000 person threshold - more than the loss experienced in the entire 1960 to 1970 decade.* Internally, moreover, the loss is shifting from the previous agricultural locus (the West North Central Division) to the industrial complexes of the East North Central Division. *The pattern in the Northeast is similar to the industrial Middle Atlantic Division buffetted by a net outmigration of over 750,000 people from 1970 to 1975.*

EXHIBIT 2-10
REGION AND DIVISION NET MIGRATION:
1960 TO 1970 AND 1970 TO 1975
(Numbers in thousands)

Region and Division	Period 1960-1970	1970-1975
Northeast Region	375	-686
Middle Atlantic Division	59	-758
New England Division	316	71
North Central Region	-752	-878
East North Central Division	-153	-774
West North Central Division	-599	-103
South Region	592	2,624
South Atlantic Division	1,332	1,859
East South Central Division	-698	202
West South Central Division	-42	563
West Region	2,854	1,467
Mountain Division	307	832
Pacific Division	2,547	635

Note: 1. Numbers may not add due to rounding.

Source: U.S. Bureau of the Census, Current Population Reports, Series P-25, No. 640, "Estimates of the Population of States with Components of Change: 1970 to 1975," U.S. Government Printing Office, Washington, D.C., 1976.

The pattern of "winners" also changes markedly. From 1960 to 1970 the West had nearly five times as many inmigrants as the South. From 1970 to 1975, the South outdistanced the West by a factor approaching two; *indeed, the entire South Region had a net inmigration of 2.6 million people - as much as the 1970 populations of Philadelphia (1.9 million) and Cleveland (751,000) combined.* Even the East South Central Division, earlier the locus of major out-movement, has been a net gainer in the last five years, as has the booming, oil rich West South Central Division.

The pattern within the West has also shifted, with the nation's former front runner, the Pacific Division, being outdistanced by the Mountain states. *To Horace Greely's earlier exhortation of "Go West Young Man" must be added an admonition - selectively! - and, based on these data, an even more overriding injunction - consider the South!* For it is not only the realities of population concentration that are rapidly being altered but also the income equivalent.

The Income Shift

As the popular media brim with accounts of Northern cities and states desperately petitioning the federal government for economic aid, it is difficult to recall the conscious policy of the United States, since the early days of the New Deal, of focusing income growth in the South. The images of tobacco road, of the dust bowl, of the share cropper, and dirt eating children have faded into the far reaches of our consciousness. It is perhaps far too easy to forget the triumph documented by the data shown in Exhibit 11: the revitalization of a region that was once America's shame.

Even as late as 1960, per capita personal incomes in the South were only about two-thirds of their Northeastern equivalents. But significant regional income homogenization has taken place during the last fifteen years. While the Northeast on this basis remains the wealthiest part of the United States, and the South still the poorest (with the West and North Central Divisions standing in the intermediate position), the relative closing of the gap is most substantial. However, differential interregional costs of living (not considered here) may serve to completely bridge the remaining spread. In the South incomes have nearly tripled in the fifteen-year period under consideration,

EXHIBIT 2-11
PER CAPITA PERSONAL INCOME CHANGE: 1960 TO 1975
(Unadjusted Dollars[1])

Region[2]	Year		Change: 1960-1975	
	1960	*1975*	*Number*	*Percent*
Northeast	$2,546	$6,305	$3,759	147.6%
North Central	2,293	6,011	3,718	162.1
South	1,760	5,148	3,388	192.5
West	2,484	6,269	3,785	152.4
U.S. TOTAL	2,222	5,834	3,612	162.6

Notes:
1. Not in constant dollars.
2. Regional incomes are population weighted means of divisional parameters. Published data only available on a division basis.

Source: U.S. Department of Commerce, Bureau of Economic Analysis, Survey of Current Business, U.S. Government Printing Office, Washington, D.C., monthly.

increasing 192.5 percent. (One should realize that
this increment in southern income levels has occurred
despite an enormous influx of retirees, many of whom
have low income, but compensatingly strong asset
positions.[3]) The Northeast had the slowest pattern of
growth, recording an increase of 147.6 percent (see
Exhibit 11).

When these data are viewed in the light of numerical
changes in total population, the potency of increased southern buying power needs little amplification.
For instance, total personal income in the South in 1975
stood at $350.7 billion, an increase of 261 percent over
the 1960 total of $97.1 billion. In contrast, the North-
east fell sharply behind the South; its 1960 total personal
income, $114.1 billion, increased by only 173 percent to
the $311.8 billion level.[4] The Northeast's lagging pace
correlates significantly with its corresponding performance
in the economic and population sectors. And this pattern
is reinforced by a key statistic related to population -
new dwelling unit starts.

Residential Construction

Any study of housing vacancy rates would certainly
mark the Northeast as a most marketable region for new
housing starts. Its vacancy rates are substantially
lower than those of the nation as a whole and, specifically, in comparison to the high growth areas of the
South and West. Yet it is the latter regions which have
consistently attracted the bulk of the new dwelling unit
starts in the country as a whole. Exhibit 12 presents
the average annual housing starts for successive three-
year increments from 1964 to 1975, with an addendum for
the first seven months of 1976. While the absolute number
of regional starts fluctuates in concert with the national
pattern of activity, *the proportional share secured by the
Northeast shows a long-term decline, from 17.8 percent
in the 1964 to 1966 period to 10.4 percent for the first
seven months of 1976.* In contrast, the South has consistently accounted for about 40 percent of the nation's
starts, despite the enormous condominium glut in Florida
during the past several years. In both cases, the pattern
of building performance is congruent to the migration and
population growth exhibited by these two regions.

EXHIBIT 2-12

RESIDENTIAL DWELLING UNIT STARTS: 1964-1976
(Numbers in thousands; Numbers represent Annual Average Starts for the Periods Indicated)

Period	U. S. Total	Northeast Region	North Central Region	South Region	West Region
1964-1966	1,422.2	253.2	337.5	553.8	277.7
1967-1969	1,455.6	224.3	359.2	589.4	282.8
1970-1972	1,977.3	276.4	395.5	860.1	445.3
1973-1975	1,527.1	203.9	352.5	638.3	332.5
1976[1]	863.5	90.2	218.3	331.0	223.5
		Percent Distribution			
1964-1966	100.0	17.8	23.7	38.9	19.5
1967-1969	100.0	15.4	24.7	40.5	19.4
1970-1972	100.0	14.0	20.0	43.5	22.5
1973-1975	100.0	13.4	23.1	41.8	21.8
1976[1]	100.0	10.4	25.3	38.4	25.9

Note: 1. First seven months, preliminary.

Source: U.S. Bureau of the Census, Construction Reports, Series C20, U.S. Government Printing Office, Washington, D.C., monthly.

The significance of housing starts has many facets. Not the least of them is the importance of housing starts as a basic multiplier for the local economy, whether it is in providing jobs for construction workers, fabricators, architects, insurors, mortgage bankers, local furniture vendors, and all of those innumerable activities that cluster both directly and indirectly to housing. Its importance, therefore, as a dynamic of local growth requires little amplification. As we have suggested earlier, jobs may have attracted people, but subsequently people and their shelter demands add further impetus to economic viability. Consequently, one final area must be considered in order to complete the evaluation of regional growth cycles - population dependent employment - private nonmanufacturing and government job shifts.

PRIVATE NONMANUFACTURING EMPLOYMENT

Exhibit 13 details the long-term (1960 to 1975) changes in private nonmanufacturing employment (excluding government) on a region and division basis. The South and West, as implied by their population growth totals, are the expansion leaders, evidencing growth rates of 77.8 and 80.1 percent, respectively, in total nonmanufacturing jobs (which include the financial, insurance, and real estate; wholesale and retail trade; transportation and public utilities; service and miscellaneous; contract construction; and mining employment subsectors). The Northeast (36.5 percent) and North Central (50.6 percent) Regions again show significant lags in their growth rates.

On a divisional partition, the Middle Atlantic states are uniquely separable in terms of their low rate of expansion -- 30.2 percent. Significantly, the New England Division's performance (59.3 percent) is not severely different from that of the nation's faster growing divisions. At the leading edge of change are the Mountain states (with a 1960 to 1975 rate of increase of 91.8 percent) and the South Atlantic Division (84.1 percent).

The fifteen-year cycle, however, touching only two moments of time, conceals significant internal dynamics that are shown in Exhibit 14. The interregional gaps - particularly the Northeast versus the South - evident during the 1960 to 1965 period, narrowed perceptively during the years 1965 to 1970, a time when the national economy was operating at full

EXHIBIT 2-13
PRIVATE NONMANUFACTURING EMPLOYMENT CHANGE:
1960 TO 1975[1] BY REGION AND DIVISION
(Numbers in thousands)

Region and Division	Year		Change 1960-1975	
	1960	*1975*	*Number*	*Percent*
Northeast Region	*7,672.4*	*10,470.5*	*2,798.1*	*36.5*
Middle Atlantic Division	6,025.2	7,847.0	1,821.8	30.2
New England Division	1,647.2	2,623.5	976.3	59.3
North Central Region	*7,512.5*	*11,311.6*	*3,799.1*	*50.6*
East North Central Division	5,252.6	7,876.2	2,623.6	49.9
West North Central Division	2,259.9	3,435.4	1,175.5	52.0
South Region	*7,547.4*	*13,415.7*	*5,868.3*	*77.8*
South Atlantic Division	3,694.0	6,802.4	3,108.4	84.1
East South Central Division	1,285.5	2,243.4	957.9	74.5
West South Central Division	2,567.9	4,369.9	1,802.0	70.2
West Region	*4,326.3*	*7,792.8*	*3,466.5*	*80.1*
Mountain Division	1,113.9	2,136.5	1,022.6	91.8
Pacific Division	3,212.4	5,656.3	2,443.9	76.1
U.S. TOTAL[2]	27,058.6	42,990.6	15,932.0	58.9

Notes: 1. Employees on nonagriculture payrolls as of March of the respective years.
2. Excludes Hawaii and Alaska.

Source: U.S. Department of Labor, Bureau of Labor Statistics, Employment and Earnings, Washington, D.C.: U.S. Government Printing Office, monthly.

EXHIBIT 2-14

REGIONAL GROWTH SHARES OF PRIVATE
MANUFACTURING EMPLOYMENT CHANGE: 1960 TO 1975[1]

(Numbers in thousands)

Region	Absolute Growth Increment			Percentage Share of National Growth		
	1960–1965	1965–1970	1970–1975	1960–1965	1965–1970	1970–1975
UNITED STATES TOTAL[2]	3,713.6	6,832.2	5,386.2	100.0	100.0	100.0
Northeast Region	660.9	1,630.9	506.3	17.8	23.9	9.4
North Central Region	848.3	1,819.0	1,131.8	22.8	26.6	21.0
South Region	1,284.5	2,149.8	2,434.0	34.6	31.5	45.2
West Region	919.9	1,232.5	1,314.1	24.8	18.0	24.4

Notes:　1.　Employees on nonagriculture payrolls as of March of the respective periods.
　　　　　2.　Excludes Hawaii and Alaska.
　　　　　3.　Numbers and percents may not add due to rounding.

Source:　U.S. Department of Labor, Bureau of Labor Statistics, Employment and Earnings, Washington, D.C.:
　　　　　U.S. Government Printing Office, monthly.

force. *In the post-1970 period, the early 1960s gap is transformed into a virtual chasm, with the South's share of national growth (45.2 percent) almost five times greater than the Northeast's (9.4 percent).* Certainly, the loss of 247,300 private nonmanufacturing jobs in New York City and Philadelphia (not shown in exhibit) exaggerated the regional differentials; yet, were we to compare the Northeast and the South, excluding these two urban giants, we would find the gap not appreciably bridged.

GOVERNMENT EMPLOYMENT CHANGE

Completing the employment cycle is the governmental sector detailed in Exhibit 15, which provides total government employment change from 1960 to 1975. These gross totals do not differentiate between federal employment and its state and local equivalents and, therefore, must be viewed with caution. The South's growth rate for the fifteen-year period (87.7 percent) surpasses that of both the Northeast (66.6 percent) and North Central states (68.3 percent), and is roughly comparable to the performance of the West Region (90.6 percent). The implications of these rate increments, which are considerably smaller than those of the other employment sectors, are troublesome. Do these growth rates of government employment represent onerous tax burdens on the older regions (the Northeast and North Central states) as they attempt to mitigate the losses, or slow growth, of private economic activity? Or do they represent the belated provision of local public services to growth areas (the South and West)? Or do the differentials constitute the selective placement of federal employment, whose impact may approximate that of a basic sector industry?

Exhibit 16 provides some insight into these questions by isolating federal civilian employment for the same time period (1960 to 1975) and area partitions. The South and West clearly serve as the major focus of federal growth, reinforcing the private sector trendlines. Indeed, the South's 31.9 percent increase, paced by the South Atlantic Division, the locus of an extensive federal bureaucracy, exceeds the Northeast's 3.3 percent increase by a tenfold margin.

Intraperiod Variations

Exhibits 17 and 18 provide the intraperiod (five-year) breakdowns for the four regional areas. The

EXHIBIT 2-15
TOTAL GOVERNMENT EMPLOYMENT CHANGE:
1960 TO 1975[1] BY REGION AND DIVISION
(Numbers in thousands)

Region and Division	Year		Change 1960-1975	
	1960	1975	Number	Percent
Northeast Region	*1,936.5*	*2,225.7*	*1,298.2*	*66.6*
Middle Atlantic Division	1,478.4	2,470.8	992.4	67.1
New England Division	485.1	754.9	296.8	64.8
North Central Region	*2,199.4*	*3,700.8*	*1,501.4*	*68.3*
East North Central Division	1,479.1	2,503.5	1,024.4	69.3
West North Central Division	730.3	1,197.3	477.0	66.2
South Region	*2,620.1*	*4,918.1*	*2,298.0*	*87.7*
South Atlantic Division	1,347.1	2,662.2	1,315.1	97.6
East South Central Division	497.3	864.6	367.3	73.9
West South Central Division	775.7	1,391.3	615.6	79.4
West Region	*1,533.4*	*2,922.7*	*1,389.3*	*90.6*
Mountain Division	403.1	806.2	403.1	100.0
Pacific Division	1,130.3	2,116.5	986.2	87.3
U. S. TOTAL[2]	8,289.4	14,767.3	6,477.9	78.1

Notes: 1. Employees on nonagriculture payrolls as of March of the respective years.
2. Excludes Hawaii and Alaska

Source: U.S. Department of Labor, Bureau of Labor Statistics, Employment and Earnings, Washington, D.C.: U.S. Government Printing Office, monthly.

EXHIBIT 2-16
FEDERAL GOVERNMENT CIVILIAN EMPLOYMENT CHANGE BY REGION AND DIVISION: 1960-1975[1]
(Numbers in thousands)

Region and Division	Year		Change 1960-1975	
	1960	1975	Number	Percent
Northeast Region	475.8	491.7	15.9	3.3
Middle Atlantic Division	362.7	375.6	12.9	3.6
New England Division	113.1	116.1	3.0	2.7
North Central Region	424.0	497.4	73.4	17.3
East North Central Division	282.2	322.3	40.1	14.2
West North Central Division	141.8	175.1	33.3	23.5
South Region	845.6	1,115.3	269.7	31.9
South Atlantic Division	516.6	723.9	207.3	40.1
East South Central Division	138.3	144.8	6.5	4.7
West South Central Division	190.7	246.6	55.9	29.3
West Region	433.1	562.7	129.6	29.9
Mountain Division	128.0	181.4	53.4	41.7
Pacific Division	305.1	381.3	76.2	25.0
U.S. TOTAL[2]	2,178.5	2,667.1	488.6	22.4

Notes: 1. As of December 31 of the respective years.
2. Excludes Hawaii and Alaska.

Source: U.S. Civil Service Commission, Monthly Review of Federal Civilian Manpower Statistics, Washington, D.C.: U.S. Government Printing Office, monthly.

patterns of change of total government employment
(Exhibit 17) correspond both with the long-term (fifteen
year) dynamic and with the intraperiod variations demonstrated in the other employment categories, with but
one exception. The Northeast, in the post-1970 period,
did not manifest the downturn in government employment
that it experienced previously in the other economic
sectors. Whether this represents cause or effect - i.e.,
whether the tax burdens associated with paying for
government employment have acted as growth inhibitors,
or whether the continued expansion is a necessary complement to a faltering private sector - remains a lingering, but significant, question.

In Exhibit 18, the federal sector is again isolated.
On a regional basis, it is apparent that federal government contraction in the Northeast and North Central
states from 1970 to 1975 must aggravate the readjustments
made necessary by the lagging private sectors in these
states. In contrast, the federal expansion in the South
and West continually added to the overall matrix of
growth. Again, it is not difficult to recognize that
the baseline tendency, particularly the evidence of the
post-1970 period, is working strongly against the aging
industrial sections of the nation.

SUMMARY

New York City is enveloped in a regional dynamic
that increasingly appears much more chronic than tran-
sient. However, it is not only affected by this broader
sweep of events but also contributes heavily to it. At
one and the same time, the city is enmeshed in the
throes of two other interrelated national phenomena:
metropolitan-nonmetropolitan shifts, a development
unique to the post-1970 era; and lingering urban-suburban tensions, whose persistence has spanned several
generations. Both of these concerns will be explored
in more depth in following chapters.

Consequently, New York City is embedded in immediate (Middle Atlantic Division) and broader (Northeast
Region) contexts whose evolutionary track severely con-
strains the city's future developmental options. A
strong regional setting provides few inhibitors to
growth; however, a weak equivalent virtually precludes
the feasibility of entertaining visions of past glories.
As we turn to the intricacies of New York City's employment base, this frame of reference should not be lost in
the welter of detail.

EXHIBIT 2-17
REGIONAL GROWTH SHARES OF
TOTAL GOVERNMENT EMPLOYMENT CHANGE: 1960 TO 1975[1]
(Numbers in thousands)

Region	Absolute Growth Increment			Percentage Share of National Growth		
	1960–1965	1965–1970	1970–1975	1960–1965	1965–1970	1970–1975
UNITED STATES TOTAL[2]	1,605.4	1,865.8	1,006.7	100.0	100.0	100.0
Northeast Region	324.9	570.1	394.2	20.2	19.9	19.6
North Central Region	384.2	797.1	320.1	23.9	27.8	16.0
South Region	518.5	932.3	847.2	32.3	32.5	42.2
West Region	377.8	566.3	445.2	23.5	19.8	22.2

Notes:
1. Employees on nonagriculture payrolls as of March of the respective periods.
2. Excludes Hawaii and Alaska.
3. Numbers and percents may not add due to rounding.

Source: U.S. Department of Labor, Bureau of Labor Statistics, Employment and Earnings, Washington, D.C.: U.S. Government Printing Office, monthly.

EXHIBIT 2-18
REGIONAL GROWTH SHARES OF
FEDERAL GOVERNMENT CIVILIAN EMPLOYMENT: 1960 TO 1975[1]
(Numbers in thousands)

Region	Absolute Growth Increment			Percentage Share of National Growth		
	1960–1965	1965–1970	1970–1975	1960–1965	1965–1970	1970–1975
UNITED STATES TOTAL[2]	187.4	258.3	42.9	100.0	100.0	100.0
Northeast Region	2.4	25.9	-12.4	1.3	10.0	-28.9
North Central Region	28.4	45.8	- 0.8	15.2	17.7	- 1.9
South Region	107.3	124.0	38.4	57.3	48.0	89.5
West Region	49.3	62.6	17.7	26.3	24.2	41.3

Notes:
1. Employees on nonagriculture payrolls as of March of the respective periods.
2. Excludes Hawaii and Alaska.
3. Numbers and percents may not add due to rounding.

Source: U.S. Department of Labor, Bureau of Labor Statistics, Employment and Earnings, Washington, D.C.: U.S. Government Printing Office, monthly.

Notes

1. Wilbur Thompson, "Economic Processes and Employment
    Problems in Declining Metropolitan Areas," in
    George Sternlieb and James W. Hughes, eds., Post
    Industrial America: Metropolitan Decline and Inter-
    Regional Job Shifts (New Brunswick, N.J.: Rutgers
    University, Center for Urban Policy Research, 1976).

2. See: Robert Murray Haig and Roswell C. McCrea,
    Major Economic Factors in Metropolitan Growth and
    Arrangement Regional Survey, Vol. 1 (New York:
    Regional Plan of New York and Its Environs, 1927;
    Edgar M. Hoover and Raymond Vernon, Anatomy of a
    Metropolis (Cambridge, Mass.: Harvard University
    Press, 1959).

3. Unpublished data, Rutgers University, Center for
    Urban Policy Research, Miami Beach Study.

4. Income data obtained from U.S. Department of
    Commerce, Bureau of Economic Analysis, Survey of
    Current Business, U. S. Government Printing Office,
    Washington, D.C., monthly.

Chapter 3

NEW YORK CITY EMPLOYMENT: PAST AND PROJECTION

INTRODUCTION

How are long-term trends distinguished from short-term temporary fluctuations? This is a persistent quandry in any projection or forecasting effort that is calibrated on historic events. Certainly, if the problems of New York were limited to the exigencies of its immediate financial crisis, difficult as their resolution might be, these problems would not necessarily dominate in a forecast of the city's future. But the trendlines presented in the preceding chapter, as well as those to be examined here, speak of more substantive and determinative tendencies. It is, of course, impossible to offer a prognosis of New York City's future economic development without acknowledging substantial uncertainty. Yet some of the basic trends appear of such momentum and long-term import that their continuation is likely to dominate any other unanticipated developments.

It is the employment base that provides the essential structuring and backbone of the city's development. Increasingly, much of the social programming of the 1960s is being refocused on the issue of basic employment opportunity. While many of the interventionary devices promulgated over the past decade focused on the specific capacities of local inhabitants and the jobs that were presumed open to them, the issue of the broader pattern of general job availability is becoming the dominant social issue of our time. *Indeed, the premise of the projection model is that the mismatch between the natural growth of the labor force and the capacity of the employment base to absorb it is a crucial determinant of population migration.* Unless the level of

jobs is commensurate with the size of the potential work
force, the city will lose population or become the place
of residence for increasing numbers of citizenry who are
external to the economic system.

In this chapter, the historic pattern of economic
change will first be reviewed, both in terms of its
relationship to the nation, and to past expectations.
The final projections are then presented and their implications for population change noted.

HISTORIC EMPLOYMENT CHANGE: A 1965 TO 1975 OVERVIEW[1]

The history of the last decade indicates a national
economy whose growth patterns have tended to exclude
New York City. As shown in Exhibit 1, which details
employment change for the city and the nation across
aggregated employment categories, the gap between the
two widens perceptibly over the time periods indicated.
While New York City's total employment increased by 4.7
percent over the 1965 to 1970 period, that of the nation
increased by 16.6 percent. Although the latter's growth
rate slackened in the succeeding five years (1970 to
1975) to 8.6 percent, the city slipped into sharp decline
(-12.5 percent). A scissors effect becomes apparent,
with the trendlines diverging sharply. Indeed, this
would also be the pattern if all the employment sectors
were subjected to graphic analysis.

Within the manufacturing sector, the city experienced
an absolute decline (-7.4 percent) at the same time
(1965 to 1970) as the nation demonstrated positive growth
(7.1 percent). Over the next five years (1970 to 1975)
the erosion of the city's manufacturing base was transformed into precipitous decline (-31.1 percent) as the
national sector also evidenced contraction (-5.2 percent).

In the 1965 to 1970 period, the manufacturing losses
of New York were adequately compensated by the growth
(7.4 percent) of employment in private nonmanufacturing
activities. In the ensuing years (1970 to 1975), the
absolute level of decline (-239,800) of the nonmanufacturing sector actually surpassed that of manufacturing
(-238,400), challenging the validity of one of the more
comforting, but unwarranted, assumptions of the past
decade. New York City, it was presumed, increasingly
would have a substitution of one type of employment for
another. Indeed, there may have been some belief that
the city really would be better off with the departure
of some manufacturing activities. Certainly, their

EXHIBIT 3-1
EMPLOYMENT CHANGE, NEW YORK CITY
AND THE NATION: 1965 TO 1975[1]
(Numbers in thousands)

	Change: 1965 to 1970		Change: 1970 to 1975	
	Number	*Percent*	*Number*	*Percent*
New York City				
TOTAL	167.5	4.7	-468.9	-12.5
Manufacturing	-98.9	-11.4	-238.4	-31.1
Private Non manufacturing	165.6	7.4	-239.8	- 9.9
Government	100.8	21.8	9.3	1.7
United States				
TOTAL	10,105	16.6	6,064	8.6
Manufacturing	1,287	7.1	-1,002	- 5.2
Private Non- manufacturing	6,331	19.4	4,854	12.4
Government	2,487	24.7	2,212	17.6

Notes: 1. Nonfarm payroll employment (wage and salary)

Source: U.S. Department of Labor, Bureau of Labor Statistics, Employment and Earnings, U.S. Government Printing Office, Washington, D.C., monthly.

replacement by the communications-intensive, face-to-
face contact industries was clearly taking place, a development of obvious virtue to the cosmopolite. While
there were some who warned about the consequences of
the loss of the export role of manufacturing and its
multiplier effect, the substitution of the exportation
of business services to the balance of the nation was
casually invoked.

However, what actually happened serves as a case
example of obsolete reference frameworks persisting
beyond their capacity either to explain or to predict.
Manufacturing was of much more significance to the
city's economy and social system than had been realized,
particularly in providing the classic entry-level jobs
such as those for the relatively unskilled in the
apparel industry. Once found on Seventh Avenue, these
jobs are now in the South, if not in Taiwan or South
Korea. Indeed, as Roger Starr has expressed:

> I walk in my melancholy daze through
> the garment district of New York City,
> hoping to be knocked into by a young
> man pushing one of those hand trucks.
> It doesn't happen any more because the
> young men have gone. Our garment in-
> dustry depended on a chain of external-
> ities - the ability to push a dress
> from the button hole maker to the
> button sewer-on, from the hem stitcher
> to the collar turner. They are all
> gone.[2]

Exacerbating this belated recognition has been the
failure of substantial growth to occur in private nonmanufacturing replacement functions or, for that matter,
the lack of new economic activities to offset the decline. We are still just at the beginning of the paper-
work revolution; but even the relatively primitive state
of its current organization appears to inhibit any
growth in jobs commensurate with the vast increase in
information-processing functions. Indeed, the age of
capital intensification of data processing is finally
with us; the computer may not displace extant employees
but, once fully integrated and assimilated into functional areas of business, it provides substantial excess
capacity without having to add proportionally more manpower. *Consequently, the replacement hypothesis was
correct. What was not fully comprehended was the shrinkage in manpower associated with a finite amount of
activity as a function of the electronics revolution.*

EXHIBIT 3-2
ACTUAL NEW YORK CITY 1975 EMPLOYMENT
VERSUS VERNON-HOOVER 1975 FORECASTS
(Numbers in thousands)

	Vernon and Hoover 1975	Actual 1975
TOTAL EMPLOYMENT	4,214.0	3,275.9
Manufacturing	995.2	527.8
Private Non manufacturing	2,799.7	2,176.0
Government	419.1	572.1

Source: Raymond Vernon, <u>Metropolis</u> 1985 (Cambridge, Harvard University Press, 1960), p. 294; U.S. Department of Labor, Bureau of Labor Statistics, <u>Employment and Earnings</u>, U.S. Government Printing Office, Washington, D.C., monthly.

*The city has been losing its manufacturing employment
just as the rationalization and the automation of paper
and information handling have finally come to fruition.*

Indeed, returning to Exhibit 1, if it were not for
the rapid increase in government employment in the 1965
to 1970 period (21.8 percent), the city's overall growth
would have been negligible, and this at a time of rapid
national expansion not likely to be replicated in the
near future. And as the 1970s commenced, government
employment in New York (a 1.7 percent increase) had
little power to offset the ominous contraction of the
balance of the local economy. As we will note subsequently, the governmental cutbacks resulting from the
fiscal crisis after 1975 serve to inhibit the positive
effects of gradual stabilization of private-sector employment in the post-1975 period.

To summarize this preliminary overview of New York
City as an employment nexus, a comparison with the forecasts for 1975 of the New York Metropolitan Region Study,
made over seventeen years ago, is informative.[3] The latter,
which represented the expectations of the collective
wisdoms circa 1960, are shown in Exhibit 2, along with
the actual 1975 experience. While the data are not directly comparable, the patterns of divergence are such
as to document a reality substantially different from
that which had been envisioned. The total growth for
the city is considerably below expectations; manufacturing employment has eroded at a pace far exceeding that
which was foreseen; and the nonmanufacturing sector has
not adequately fulfilled earlier anticipations - the
post-industrial transformation has created a void only
partially bridged by nonmanfacturing employment. Only
the governmental sector has realized the projected
potential - so much so that its 1975 employment total
exceeds that of manufacturing. *The projected consequences
of the maturation of the service age have only partially materialized. Unfortunately, the major benefits
have accrued to geographic loci external to New York
City.*

The Major Sectors

Exhibits 3 and 4 provide a more comprehensive
tabulation of the absolute levels of and changes in employment for New York City and the nation over the
1965 to 1975 period. As has already been made evident
in Exhibit 1, the two five-year intervals of this period
are vastly different in character. However, it should

EXHIBIT 3-3
NEW YORK CITY EMPLOYMENT CHANGE: 1965 TO 1975[1]
(Numbers in thousands)

	1965	1970	1975	Change: 1965–1970 Number	Percent	Change: 1970–1975 Number	Percent	Change: 1965–1975 Number	Percent
Total	3577.3	3744.8	3275.9	167.5	4.7	-468.9	-12.5	-301.4	-8.4
Mining	2.4	1.9	1.5	- .5	-20.8	- 0.4	-21.1	- 0.9	-37.5
Construction	109.2	110.1	77.9	0.9	0.8	- 32.2	-29.2	-31.3	-28.7
Manufacturing	865.1	766.2	527.8	-98.9	-11.4	-238.4	-31.1	-337.3	-39.0
Transportation and Public Utilities	318.4	323.3	268.4	4.9	1.5	- 54.9	-17.0	- 50.0	-15.7
Wholesale and Retail Trade	747.7	735.5	635.3	-12.2	- 1.6	-100.2	-13.6	-112.4	-18.5
Wholesale Trade	310.1	302.0	252.7	- 8.1	- 2.6	- 49.3	-16.3	- 57.4	-18.5
Retail Trade	437.6	433.5	382.6	- 4.1	- 0.9	- 50.9	-11.7	- 55.0	-12.6
Finance, Insurance, and Real Estate	391.4	459.6	422.1	68.2	17.4	- 37.5	- 8.2	30.7	7.8
Services	681.1	785.4	770.7	104.3	15.3	- 14.7	- 1.9	89.6	13.2
Government	462.0	562.8	572.1	100.8	21.8	9.3	1.7	110.1	23.8
Federal	112.5	107.5	91.4	- 5.0	- 4.4	- 16.1	-15.0	-21.1	-18.8
State and Local	349.5	455.3	480.7	105.8	30.3	25.4	5.6	131.2	37.5
State	NA	40.9	47.9	-	-	7.0	17.1	-	-
Local	NA	414.4	432.8	-	-	18.4	4.4	-	-

Notes   1. Nonfarm payroll employment, annual average.

Source: U.S. Department of Labor, Bureau of Labor Statistics, Employment and Earnings, U.S. Government Printing Office Washington, D.C., monthly.

EXHIBIT 3-4
UNITED STATES EMPLOYMENT CHANGE: 1965-1975[1]
(Numbers in thousands)

	1965	1970	1975	Change:1965-1970 Number	Percent	Change:1970-1975 Number	Percent	Change:1965-1975 Number	Percent
TOTAL	60,816	70,921	76,985	10,105	16.6	6,064	8.6	16,169	26.6
Mining	632	623	745	- 9	- 1.4	122	19.6	113	17.9
Construction	3,186	3,536	3,457	350	11.0	- 79	- 2.2	271	8.5
Manufacturing	18,062	19,349	18,347	1,287	7.1	-1,002	- 5.2	285	1.6
Transportation and Public Utilities	4,036	4,504	4,498	468	11.6	- 6	- .1	462	11.4
Wholesale and Retail Trade	12,716	15,040	16,947	2,324	18.3	1,907	12.7	4,231	33.3
Finance, Insurance, and Real Estate	3,023	3,687	4,223	664	22.0	536	14.5	1,200	39.7
Services	9,087	11,621	13,995	2,534	27.9	2,374	20.4	4,908	54.0
Government	10,074	12,561	14,773	2,487	24.7	2,212	17.6	4,699	46.6

Notes: 1. Nonfarm payroll employment, annual average.

Source: U.S. Department of Labor, Bureau of Labor Statistics, Employment and Earnings, U.S. Government Printing Office, Washington, D.C., monthly.

also be noted that the full scale of the transition is obscured, since the year 1969 marks the actual break in trend. For example, the total employment level of the city increased from 3.58 million jobs in 1965 to 3.74 million in 1970 (Exhibit 3), and then descended to the 3.28 million mark by 1975. But in 1969, the employment total reached 3.80 million jobs; if this year were used to partition the ten-year period, the ascent and fall of the city's economy would be even more accentuated. Nonetheless, since the patterns are not obscured by the five-year convention, we will hold to these intervals.

In 1965, manufacturing was still the dominant sector of New York City's employment base (865,100 jobs). As a point of reference, there were over one million manufacturing jobs recorded in each of the years between 1947 and 1957. By 1975, 527,800 manufacturing jobs remained. Sequentially expanding the observational time frame, the following patterns of decline emerge: between 1970 and 1975, -238,400 jobs; between 1965 and 1975, -337,300 jobs; and between 1947 and 1975, -545,100 jobs (there were 1,072,900 manufacturing jobs in the city in 1947).

Certainly, the long-term trend had not been ignored in the classic expositions on the city's economy. For example, Vernon and Hoover correctly noted that "there is no prospect, short of some new forces of major dimensions, that this incipient decline will be arrested in the decades ahead."[4] Yet new forces did surface, only to transform what had been a livable slow erosion of the city's manufacturing base into something of a major crisis. The pyramiding effects of the regional shift, creating in the growth areas of the country the critical mass of population necessary for import substitution to occur, which in complementary fashion, initiated a declining export role for New York; the sudden redefinition of the entire energy matrix, which has bestowed increasing competitive advantage to the nation's energy exporting territories, and the just recently acknowledged phenomenon, the growth of manufacturing in the lesser developed countries (LDCs) particularly in the Far East, whose full market penetration has yet to be clarified; all converged in the early 1970s to exacerbate what had been a gradual decline in the city's role as a manufacturing nexus.

As we look to the future, these forces appear to represent endemic parameters; the major question is whether their full impact has already been absorbed. Or is there some minimum baseline level of activity that

will persist by virtue of the city's unique attributes,
the captive market it represents (the city and the region
are still influential market areas despite the myth and
reality of Sunbelt affluence), and the forces wielded
by historical inertia (activities wedded to their present location simply because that's where they always
have been). These concerns will be returned to as the
projections are subsequently examined.

The white-collar industries - transportation and
public utilities; trade; finance, insurance, and real
estate; and services - constitute the private-employment
sectors central to the post-industrial transformation.
Communications-oriented, information-dependent and adja-
cent functions depending on face-to-face contact and
immediate access to "what's going on" had been assumed
to be the true growth sectors of the city. Indeed,
Hoover and Vernon suggested:

> Face to face interchange is the only
> adequate means of communication for
> much of the ... work of ... executives...
> the business elite ... and the finan-
> cial community; ... delicate negotia-
> tions and subtle, complex ideas are not
> easily entrusted to the telephone or the
> letter. In this respect ... Manhattan...
> has a clear advantage over any other
> location.[5]

But the communications revolution, the continued evolution of the nation's transportation system, and the
gravitation of the nation's decisionmaking apparatus
to Washington, have challenged these assumptions.

Certainly, the financial and service sectors per-
formed as expected through 1970 (positive growth) but,
in the ensuing five-year period, both were afflicted
with declines. Wholesale and retail trade, long viewed
as impregnable accompaniments of New York's market
dominance, saw slow erosion in the 1965 to 1970 period
(-1.6 percent) transformed into a major downturn in
the post-1970 years (-13.6 percent). Transportation and
public utilities experienced a somewhat more severe
reversal, slipping from moderate growth (1.5 percent)
in the first five years (1965 to 1970) to sharp decline
in the early portions of the 1970s (-17.0 percent).
Consequently, the performance of the combined nonmanufacturing sectors, rather than serving to buffer the
manufacturing losses, contributed to the overall matrix
of decline. Indeed, their effect is nowhere better

documented than in the construction industry, with employment losses of 32,200 jobs (-29.2 percent) between
1970 and 1975.

The Governmental Sector

It is government employment that has served as the
dominant locus of growth in New York City over the 1965
to 1975 period, securing an increase of 110,100 jobs.
However, the gains have been the province of the state
and local sector, with federal employment showing a
marked withdrawal over the ten-year period (-21,100
jobs). The latter development is particularly signfi-
cant since its economic effect approximates that of a
basic sector industry, i.e., its support accrues from
external sources, drawing into the city an income flow
that has a very significant multiplier effect on the
urban economy generally. As the data in Exhibit 3
affirm, the shrinking federal role has been more than
compensated by the local sectors in terms of absolute
numbers of jobs; but to the degree that the latter are
not supported by external transfer payments, their
secondary effects are not of comparable import.

The Constant Share Gap

Two other brief analyses are appropriate in completing the historical inventory. The first is summarized in Exhibit 5, in which a comparison is made
between the actual 1975 employment level in New York
City and that which would have accrued if the city
maintained its 1965 share of national employment through
1975, i.e., a hypothetical 1975 employment total algebraically defined as follows:

$$E_{1975}^{ic} = \frac{E_{1965}^{ic}}{E_{1965}^{in}} \cdot E_{1975}^{in}$$

where E = employment
      i = industrial category
      c = New York City
      n = nation

If New York had secured a constant share of the national
growth between 1965 and 1975, the city's total employment in 1975 would have been 4.6 million jobs instead
of the actual 3.3 million; the employment gap because
of differential growth rates exceeded 1.3 million jobs.

EXHIBIT 3-5
ACTUAL 1975 NEW YORK CITY EMPLOYMENT VERSUS HYPOTHESIZED CONSTANT SHARE ALTERNATIVE

	Actual 1975 Employment	Constant Share 1975 Employment	Constant Share Gap
Total	3,275.9	4,624.6	-1,348.7
Mining	1.5	2.8	- 1.3
Construction	77.9	118.5	- 40.6
Manufacturing	527.8	878.7	- 350.9
Transportation and Public Utilities	268.4	354.8	- 86.4
Wholesale and Retail Trade	635.3	996.5	- 361.2
Finance, Insurance, and Real Estate	422.1	546.8	- 124.7
Services	770.7	1,049.0	- 278.3
Government	572.1	677.5	- 105.4

Source: Base data, Exhibits 3 and 4.

The latter figure can be construed as the job loss stem-
ming from the city's competitive disadvantages; in terms
of shift-share analysis, it can be considered a competitive component.

Whatever the terminology, every major industrial
sector in the city exhibits an employment shortfall,
with wholesale and retail trade (361,200 jobs) and manufacturing (350,900 jobs) demonstrating the weakest competitive positions. When considered in conjunction with
the gaps attached to the entire profile, the myth of the
growth in exportation of higher valued administrative
services (as manufacturing replacement activities) is
readily exposed.

The Decline in Self-Employment

The second analysis centers about a category of
employment not encompassed by the preceding data tabulations. As noted before, the analyses to this point have
been based on standardized nonfarm wage and salary
(payroll) employment tabulations of the Bureau of Labor
Statistics, which exclude self-employed and unpaid
family workers. For illustrative purposes, Exhibit 6
provides a comparison between wage and salary employment and total employment for New York City for 1960
and 1970, with total employment incorporating estimates
of self-employed and unpaid family workers - the province of small-scale entrepreneurs.[6]

What is strikingly evident in the data is the decline in the latter over time. If wage and salary employment is first considered, a growth increment of
over 206,000 jobs is apparent. However, translation
into a total employment equivalent finds the growth
total reduced to 45,000. *Hence the conventional wage
and salary tabulations tend to overestimate growth and
understate decline - longitudinally, the percentage of
self-employed in every industry category has declined
markedly.* For the period denoted here, part of the
process of change encompasses the phenomenon of self-
employed workers becoming part of the wage and salary
base, as well as the actual demise of independent
entrepreneurs.

This evolution may render yet another notion obsolete - the incubator hypothesis. It has been
assumed traditionally that the dense matrix and pool
of activities and services in urban locations - the
chain of externalities - hatched new industries. The
city would house small new struggling businesses, many
individually owned; though a great proportion either

EXHIBIT 3-6
WAGE AND SALARY VS. TOTAL EMPLOYMENT, NEW YORK CITY: 1960 TO 1970
(Numbers in thousands)

| | *WAGE AND SALARY EMPLOYMENT* | | | |
| | | | *Change: 1960 to 1970* | |
	1960	*1970*	*Number*	*Percent*
Total	3,538.4	3,744.8	206.4	5.8
Mining	1.9	1.9	0.0	0.0
Construction	125.3	110.1	- 15.2	-12.1
Manufacturing	946.8	766.2	-180.6	-19.1
Transportation and Public Utilities	318.1	323.3	5.2	1.6
Wholesale and Retail Trade	744.8	735.5	- 9.3	- 1.2
Finance, Insurance, and Real Estate	386.0	459.6	73.6	19.1
Services	607.3	785.4	178.1	29.3
Government	408.2	562.8	154.6	37.9

	TOTAL EMPLOYMENT			
Total	3,954.1	3,999.1	45.0	1.1
Mining	2.0	2.0	0.0	0.0
Construction	163.3	130.0	-33.3	-20.4
Manufacturing	967.0	775.8	-191.2	-19.8
Transportation and Public Utilities	332.8	334.2	1.4	0.4
Wholesale and Retail Trade	918.0	811.8	-106.2	-11.6
Finance, Insurance and Real Estate	418.7	483.1	64.4	15.4
Services	744.1	899.4	155.3	20.9
Government	408.2	562.8	154.6	37.9

Source: U.S. Department of Labor, Bureau of Labor Statistics, Employment and Earnings, U.S. Government Printing Office, Washington, D.C. monthly (base wage and salary data).

would not survive or would plateau, a significant segment would evolve into the giants of the future. While
the latter would move away when production became rou-
tinized and standardized, continued innovation would
always provide a set of replacement activities and jobs.

The data in Exhibit 6 are far from sanguine on this
assumption; moreover, other processes of significant
scope are suggested, particularly in the case of wholesale and retail trade. While wage and salary employment
declined by 9,300 jobs in this sector, the decline in
total employment in the wholesale and retail trade was
well over 106,000. Much of this differential comprises
small-scale retailing, which at one time provided an
essential stepping stone to capital accumulation and
middle-class status for wave after wave of upwardly
mobile migrants to the city. The empty stores of
Brownsville, and the South Bronx, and the sad realities
of the empty sandwich bars in the old loft buildings
bespeak the substantial lessening of this mode of opportunity within the city.

Nonetheless, the major point to be stressed by this
comparison is that it is possible for total employment
to remain constant while wage and salary employment
registers gains - a byproduct of the declining national
economic role of self-employment. Additionally, while
not all small-scale entrepreneurs are encompassed by
this classification, it is important to note that the
great bulk of the industrial loft structures of New
York have catered to relatively small independent firms.
The evolution to larger scale corporate formats, particularly in retailing, appears to have had significant
ramifications for manufacturing in the city; certainly
the vacation of multistoried industrial parcels can be,
at least partially, ascribed to this phenomenon.

The More Recent Pattern

As of this writing, the United States is well into
its third year of recovery from the abrupt recession of
1974. How has New York City fared in the period following 1975, the final reporting year of the preceding
analyses? The data of Exhibit 7 provide some answers
to this question, delineating average annual employment
totals for 1975 and 1976, and for the first six months
of 1977. While two years are certainly not sufficient
in and of themselves to counteract the tendencies of
the preceding decade, the image they record is cause
for guarded optimism.

EXHIBIT 3-7
NEW YORK CITY EMPLOYMENT CHANGE: 1975 TO 1977[1]
(Numbers in thousands)

	1975	1976	1977[2]	Change: 1975 to 1977 Number	Change: 1975 to 1977 Percent
Total	3,275.9	3,188.3	3,149.5	-126.4	- 3.9
Mining	1.5	1.6	1.7	0.2	13.3
Construction	77.9	71.7	63.1	- 14.8	- 19.0
Manufacturing	527.8	524.8	536.2	8.4	1.6
Transportation and Public Utilities	268.4	262.0	259.1	- 9.3	- 3.5
Wholesale and Retail Trade	635.3	629.1	620.6	-14.7	- 2.3
Finance, Insurance, and Real Estate	422.1	417.9	414.6	- 7.5	- 1.8
Services	770.7	764.2	766.3	- 4.4	- 0.6
Government	572.1	517.0	487.9	-84.2	- 14.7
Federal	91.4	86.3	84.4	- 7.0	- 7.7
State	47.9	46.3	47.5	- 0.4	- 0.8
Local	432.8	384.4	356.0	-76.8	- 17.7

Notes: 1. Nonagricultural payroll employment, annual average.
2. Average, first six months of 1977.

Source: U.S. Department of Labor, Bureau of Labor Statistics, Employment and Earnings, U.S. Government Printing Office, Washington, D.C. monthly.

The reversals emanating from the fiscal crisis impacted the city in the 1975 to 1977 period. The immediate effect is the sharp downturn in local government employment, terminating a long-term trend of consistent growth. *Indeed, absent this sector, the overall city economy appears on the verge of impending stabilization. Certainly it must be realized that this has taken place in the context of vigorous national growth; but if it reflects more than a brief interlude, the comparison with the recent past is somewhat encouraging. At the very least, the rapid pace of shrinkage has been substantially alleviated.* The major question is whether the long-term trendlines are etched so deeply that they will reassert themselves if the national economy falters.

THE PROJECTIONS: 1975 to 1985

In Exhibit 8 are presented the employment projections for New York City for 1980 and 1985. Again, at the risk of redundancy, a note of clarification is required. The projections are cast in terms of total employment, including self-employed and unpaid family workers, and are not directly comparable to the bulk of the preceding statistical presentations. This intermixture of alternative employment formulations is perhaps unavoidable. The national projections, the initial data input into three of the four models, comprise total employment, requiring the city projections to be of a consistent format. All of the preceding analyses, in contrast, used wage and salary employment, the actual unit of measurement of the standardized reporting and accounting systems. The latter facilitated uniform and consistent comparisons both over time and between areas.

The full projection methodology has been presented in Chapter Two. To reiterate: the output of the separate models has been averaged to derive what is termed the central projection. About this measure of central tendency, an indication of the dispersion of the separate projections has been calculated (via procedures analogous to computing a mean deviation), deriving what we term a band of likelihood. In Exhibit 8, the center column under the 1980 and 1985 headings is the central projection, with the flanking columns delineating the range within which there is a considerable likelihood of future reality. One should not interpret this as a claim to statistical reliability; our terminology may imply a level of exactitude that

EXHIBIT 3-8

NEW YORK CITY EMPLOYMENT PROJECTIONS: 1975 TO 1985

(Numbers in thousands)

	1975	1980 High	1980 Central Projection	1980 Low	1985 High	1985 Central Projection	1985 Low
Total	3,498.9	3,484.8	3,285.9	3,087.0	3,534.6	3,212.6	2,890.6
Mining	1.5	1.7	1.6	1.5	1.7	1.5	1.3
Construction	92.0	87.7	73.7	59.7	93.1	76.9	60.7
Manufacturing	534.4	556.5	514.5	472.5	559.5	475.6	391.7
Transportation and Public Utilities	277.4	280.1	256.7	233.3	283.0	247.8	212.6
Wholesale and Retail Trade	695.1	703.5	663.4	623.3	709.4	644.2	579.0
Finance, Insurance, and Real Estate	443.7	464.3	438.1	411.9	491.7	445.0	398.3
Services	882.6	899.1	876.5	853.9	932.8	896.2	859.6
Government	572.1	491.9	461.4	430.9	463.4	425.4	387.4
Federal	91.4	77.8	75.5	73.2	64.4	60.6	56.8
State	47.9	47.9	50.2	52.5	55.6	53.0	50.4
Local	432.8	366.2	335.7	305.2	343.4	311.8	280.2

Source: CUPR Projections.

is simply not warranted.

With these admonitions in mind, the central projections define a future path that represents a dampening of past trendlines. While we do not envision a
major deflection or reversal of the patterns documented
over the 1965 to 1975 period, their severity should be
considerably muted. As shown in Exhibit 8, the 1975
employment total (3.50 million jobs) is projected to
decline to 3.29 million jobs by 1980, a shift far less
precipitous than that of the preceding five years.
And in a continuing abatement of the scale of decline,
the projected total for 1985 stands at the 3.21 million
job mark. Consequently, the total employment loss projected over the 1975 to 1985 period is 286,000 jobs,
the bulk of which are registered in the first five years.

The broad range of future eventualities is defined
by an upper boundary representing abrupt stabilization,
with total employment fluctuating in the vicinity of
3.5 million jobs over the ten-year projection interval.
In contrast, the lower boundary initially approximates
a simple extension of the 1970 to 1975 trendline, with
3.09 million jobs projected for 1980. Then, it too
begins to level off, resulting in a 1985 employment
total of 2.89 million jobs. Consequently, the projection band traces out a broad future path, ever widening
but veering away from the sharp gradient characteristic
of the early 1970s (see Exhibit 9). The ceiling (upper
limit) defines immediate stabilization while the floor
(lower limit) may portend a longer term transformation
to a much lower, but also stabilized, plane of economic
activity. Certainly the probable range broadens as
the projection span lengthens; nonetheless, the central
projection will represent the working hypothesis for
the succeeding portions of this study. Therefore, as
we turn to the specific industrial sectors, discussion
will be directed mainly toward the central projections.

Employment in the *mining sector* is expected to
undergo minimal change, maintaining approximately 1500
jobs for the duration (Exhibit 8). *Construction,* of
much greater visibility, particularly as it is manifested
in an evolving cityscape, is dependent on the performance and needs of the balance of the industry profile,
the supply of underutilized physical facilities, and
the scale of governmental inputs. As such, construction employment is projected to decline from 92,000
jobs in 1975 to 73,700 by 1980, and then exhibits a
modest recovery over the 1980 to 1985 period.

EXHIBIT 3-9
PROJECTION BAND: 1970 TO 1985

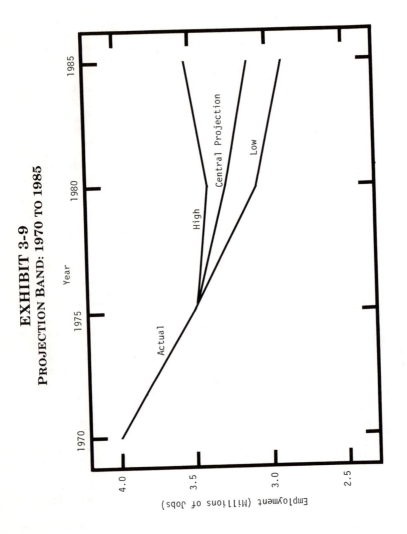

Source: Exhibit B

The projection of *manufacturing employment* is particularly problematic, affected as it is by a chain of events beyond the limits of New York City. Can "hard" products destined for territories outside the city's borders be produced competitively, particularly in light of the same question facing the United States in relation to the international arena? Of equal significance to both of these domestic political jurisdictions is the question of whether they are competitive in manufacturing products designed for consumption within their immediate domains. *It seems to us that the major problem facing New York is not how much new activity it can attract, but how much of its existing base can it retain.* Its future level of manufacturing employment, then, may well be defined by its basic retention capacity; in turn, this will certainly pivot on the capacity of the city's public policy and labor sectors to react to a diminishing competitive posture.

It is beyond our capacity to precisely prognosticate the resolution and outcome of this matrix of uncertainties. As evidence of the impossibility of this task stands the very width of the band of manufacturing projections presented in Exhibit 8. Nonetheless, the central projection portends a continuing erosion of this sector, with the decline of 20,000 jobs over the 1975 to 1980 period standing as a brief respite before somewhat more substantial losses accrue in the early 1980s. By 1985, the absolute level of employment is projected at 475,600 jobs. This represents a substantial abatement in the severity of past trendlines and may well be indicative of the approach toward some minimum threshold base of manufacturing activity.

Transportation and public utilities will continue to endure slow but persistent declines; however, there is some indication of impending stability in the latter stages of the projection interval. Over the 1975 to 1985 period the level of employment is projected to decline from 277,500 jobs to 247,800, with two-thirds of the loss of 29,700 jobs absorbed in the first five years under consideration.

Wholesale and retail trade is another sector whose future is linked closely to the concept of competitiveness, particularly on a metropolitan scale. Ignoring changes in the absolute size of consumer spending flows and shifting manpower requirements as functional operations become more capital intensive (instantaneous accounts receivable posting and the like), employment levels are dependent on market share capture. Even if

residential populations were wedded to their present
loci, the continued rise of alternative facilities and
opportunities would challenge the extant infrastructure
of New York City. In the past, the city has reflected
such market inroads by a process of gradual secular
declines. Dramatic short-term (1970-1975) contractions
have probably been linked to more fundamental disruptions
of the post-1970 years - sharp population and economic
declines. Were the latter to stabilize, the increasing
critical mass of suburban alternatives might still continue to erode the city's market penetration. In this
context, the central projection is one of gradually
tapering decline, with wholesale and retail trade employment losing approximately 50,000 jobs over the ten
years under consideration - from 695,100 in 1975 to
644,200 in 1985.

In contrast, the *finance, insurance, and real estate,
and service* components of the city's economic base -
activities destined as major growth sectors in an evolving
national economy - may serve as bulwarks in a long-term
holding action by the city. The central projections indicate a strong potential for employment stabilization
in these activities, with the 1980 and 1985 job totals
fluctuating about that of the base year (1975). Indeed,
success in basic job retention in New York will probably
hinge to a considerable degree on these two employment
sectors.

The preceding elements of New York's economy can
be construed as private sector activities, although
their underlying support in several cases may well depend on infusions of government resources. If they are
aggregated, what future do they portend? The gross
totals are as follows:

Total Private Employment

1975	2,926,800
1980	2,824,500
1985	2,787,200

*The central projections, while far from ebullient,
herald a return to a more manageable transition, providing the city with the opportunity to effectively
adjust to a new baseline.*

The capacity of government employment to effectuate
or buffer this evolution has been depleted. The full
ramifications of its overextension in compensating for
past economic lags have become evident - in shoring
up the past, growth was borrowed from the future. As

we have entered into that future, the city, subject
to federal policy, confronts negative governmental
growth, dampening the glimmers of potential stabilization.

The forecasting of government employment poses areas
of great uncertainty. The 1975 to 1977 data have already documented the traumatic adjustments fostered by
the fiscal crisis. Clearly, the final arbiters of this
saga will set the parameters of the future; what eventualities will ensue are outside the range of all but
the most omniscient seer. Yet the central projections
do provide a scenario that, at least for the short term,
appears plausable. It is one of contracting local government employment, the continuing erosion of the federal
sector, and a slowly growing state equivalent. While
overall declines are projected to persist through 1985 -
with total government employment falling from 572,100
jobs in 1975 to 425,000 in 1985 - the more severe
effects should be absorbed by 1980. Nonetheless, government employment will probably trend toward the level
extant in 1960 - slightly above the 400,000 job threshold.

SUMMARY

The economy of New York City has always been
dominated by change. Yet, it continued to adapt and
thrive while evolving rapidly in format and composition.
For example, measured in terms of total employment
(including self-employed and unpaid family workers),
the following changes were experienced.

1. Between 1960 and 1970, the total employment
   of the city remained virtually constant, increasing from 3.95 million to 4.00 million
   jobs. However, its major industrial sectors
   experienced a great deal of flux.

     a) Manufacturing employment declined by
        19.8 percent, or 191,200 jobs. Si-
        milarly, the wholesale and retail
        trade sector lost 11.6 percent of the
        1960 employment base (-106,200 jobs).

     b) At the same time, there was compensat-
        ing growth in other industrial sectors.
        Finance, insurance, and real estate
        secured an additional 64,400 jobs (15.4
        percent); services accrued a gain of
        155,300 jobs (20.9 percent); and govern-
        ment expanded by 154,600 jobs (37.9
        percent).

     c) Over the 1960 to 1970 period, substi-
        tution was characteristic of the city's
        economy, as it adapted to the post-indus-
        trial transformation and the emerging
        service era.

2. That this overall stability was maintained only
   in the context of a vigorous national economy
   evoked only little concern. When the latter
   faltered in the 1970 to 1975 period, and the
   new regional and energy realities took hold,
   a fundamental transformation was produced in
   the city's economy. The process of change was
   no longer one of compensation; rather it was
   one of painful shrinkage.

     a) From 1970 to 1975, the total employment
        of the city declined by over 500,000
        jobs or -12.5 percent (again measured
        in terms of total employment, including
        self-employed; see Exhibits 6 and 8).

b) Over this period, manufacturing losses exceeded 241,000 jobs (-31.1 percent), an acceleration of past trendlines. However, the private nonmanufacturing sector could not longer counterbalance this loss as it too contributed to the matrix of decline, losing 268,100 jobs (-10.1 percent).

c) And no longer could growth in government employment sustain a faltering private sector. Its employment growth was only 9,300 jobs (1.7 percent).

3. Over the 1975 to 1977 period, evidence is mounting that the painful process of erosion is beginning to abate. However, the fiscal crisis has hindered the transition to stability - the governmental sector lost 84,200 jobs (-14.7 percent) over this period.

4. The band of projections through 1985 encompasses several possible scenarios. The upper boundary defines immediate stability at the 3.5 million job level, the same as that of 1975. The lower boundary projects continued employment losses, but at a decreasing rate over time. Stability is approached, but at a much lower plane - at less than 2.9 million jobs.

5. The central projection, however, represents the immediate working hypothesis of the balance of the study. It defines a path of slow erosion - relative to the 1970 to 1975 experience - with the 1985 projection standing at just over 3.2 million jobs. The bulk of the losses that are expected to accrue between 1975 and 1985 (286,300) are registered in the first five years of this period.

6. The individual industry sectors exhibit varied patterns of behavior.

a) Consistent with 1975 to 1977, but contrary to the fifteen previous years, the governmental sector is projected to lose over 146,000 jobs between 1975 and 1985, accounting for over half of the city's total decline.

b) Manufacturing is also expected to decline throughout the ten-year projection

span (-58,800 jobs) but at a rate far
less precipitous than that of the recent
past.

c) Significantly, private nonmanufacturing
employment, while in total reflecting
stability, shows little capacity to compensate for the expected losses in the
manufacturing and governmental sectors.
The job intensive opportunities of the
post-industrial transformation are bypass-
ing New York City.

7. The central projection indicates that the magnitude of the transition, though negative, is
limited and thus may permit the city to effectively adjust to its main thrust. While it provides little evidence for complacency, it also
gives little reason for despair. Certainly, the
potential of public policy inputs yielding significant dividends is present. But only if the
political will is certain.

LABOR FORCE DEMAND

Changes in employment levels in and of themselves
require structuring to provide insight into their implications for population changes. However, the pattern
of job decline evidenced below suggest a lowering of
any population base predicated on the 1970 economic level.

Year (Period)	Employment Level	Intraperiod Change
1970	3,999,100	
(1970-1975)		-500,200
1975	3,498,900	
(1975-1980)		-213,000
1980	3,285,900	
(1980-1985)		- 73,300
1985	3,212,600	

Yet, a host of intervening factors are operative. The
translation of employment changes into labor force demand
(LFD) consequences relates to the following concerns:

1. Multiple jobholders

2. The share of New York City jobs secured by the city's residents

3. The scale of reverse commutation, i.e., New York City residents employed outside the city

4. The unemployment rate, whose statistical complement (1 - employment rate) translates employment to labor force, i.e., labor force equals the employed plus unemployed

These factors have exhibited conflicting patterns of variation in the past, thereby requiring forecasts for use in each of the projection periods. Of critical importance in this context is the unemployment rate. For example, suppose 3,000,000 jobs are held by New York City residents, and the unemployment rate is 4.8 percent. Therefore, the size of the labor force equals:

$$\frac{3,000,000}{1 - .048} = 3,151,261 = \text{labor force}$$

If the unemployment rate is 10.6 percent, a far larger labor force is implied:

$$\frac{3,000,000}{1 - .106} = 3,355,705 = \text{labor force}$$

In the model, the following unemployment rates have been used, with the 1970 and 1975 rates being those actually experienced, while the 1980 and 1985 equivalents are projections.

Year	Unemployment Rate (percent)
1970	4.8
1975	10.6
1980	15.0
1985	15.0

The reasonableness of the 1980 and 1985 projections is based upon the analysis presented at the end of Chapter 5. The increase in the youthfulness of the labor force combined with the high level of minority group unemployment, absent migration, tend to make a higher unemployment rate not unreasonable. Undoubtedly, the phenomenon could well be absorbed by individuals dropping out of the labor force, thereby altering the pattern of labor-force participation rates. While projections of the latter are undertaken in the population (supply) analysis, the adjustments fostered by mismatches between supply and demand are mainly reflected in our employment-rate projections.

As a result of these assumptions and the projections of the ancilliary factors noted previously, the forecasts of the employment demand (jobs available for New York City residents) and labor force demand (employment demand divided by the employment rate complement) are as follows:

Year	Resident Employment Demand	Labor Force Demand
1970	3,202,906	3,364,397
1975	2,885,997	3,228,185
1980	2,790,694	3,283,169
1985	2,781,472	3,272,320

It is the labor force demand that, when compared to the labor force supply (LFS) - the latter derived from cohort survival analysis of the city's population - establishes the base magnitude of the migration variable. As the following chapters will show, the labor supply for each projection interval exceeds the projected demand, generating outmigration. It is to the population analysis that attention is now directed.

Notes

1. It is important to stress that the employment data of this chapter are expressed as annual averages. In the preceding chapter, the employment data were measured as of March of the respective years. Consequently, there will be some slight discrepancies in the totals for comparable years.

2. Roger Starr, "The Dilemmas of Governmental Responses," George Sternlieb and James W. Hughes, eds., Post Industrial America: Metropolitan Decline and Inter-Regional Job Shifts (New Brunswick, N.J., Rutgers University, Center for Urban Policy Research, 1976), p. 248.

3. Edgar M. Hoover and Raymond Vernon, Anatomy of a Metropolis (Cambridge, Harvard University Press, 1959).

4. Ibid., p. 57.

5. Ibid., p. 97.

6. Total employment was determined by use of multipliers secured from the industry-class of worker matrix from the decennial census.

Chapter 4

THE POPULATION CONTEXT:
NEW YORK CITY AND THE NATION

INTRODUCTION

The metropolitan landscapes of America bear testi-
mony to the effects of the evolution and transformation
of the nation's population. The old- and new-law tenements of New York City, for example, serve to document
the waves of overseas inmigration buffeting the nation
in the decades bounding the turn of the century.[1] Like-
wise, the inner bands of single-family suburbia surround-
ing the city serve as a reminder of the great postwar
baby boom, when, in a twenty-year period (1945 to 1965),
America's population increased by 54 million people.[2]
And, as a reflection of more contemporary events, stand
the broad stretches of inner-city housing abandonment
which are physical residuals of the decline of immigration
from abroad, of the depletion of the pool of rural agricultural displacees, and of the unrestrained population
flows terminating originally in nearby suburbia but,
more recently, in a marked amplification of scale, shifting to the lures of the Sunbelt.

This seemingly remorseless sequence of national
events, however, is not only gauged by physical correlates but also expressed in distinct urban social com-
positions, which, as they interact with succeeding
national phenomena, in turn tend to modify and refine
the impacts of the latter.

In the future, then, alterations in the parameters
of the national population promise to etch deeply not
only into the physical fabric of the nation's cities
but also into the foundations of their demography.
Yet, at the same time, the historical precedents, both
national and local, bear a considerable life force of

their own, intersecting the trajectories of present and future population swings. Consequently, the task of this chapter is to examine the patterns of population change in New York City in the recent past, their correlation to their national counterparts, and - in order to establish a set of baseline future expectations - to examine the national population trendlines that can be anticipated with some degree of certainty.

THE SETTING

In analyzing and projecting population - even more than in most other social phenomena - a substantial portion of the future is essentially cast by the parameters of the past. Subject to migration, for example, future population change is constrained to the maturation of the past base population and its pattern of fertility. In the context of formal projection methodology (absent migration), the future is elaborated as a function of age-specific survival and birth rates applied to the historical age structure of the population. Even when migration - the more volatile component of population change - is considered, it too is linked to its historical record. At a minimum, the outlines of the recent past provide at least some baseline expectation of the contours of the future.

Moreover, similar to many other socioeconomic phenomena, the population trends of local jurisdictions are intertwined with national dynamics and trendlines. For example, national patterns of fertility, while modified by local variations, are substantially reflected at lower geographical scales. New York City's future population is not only a prisoner of its historical past but also is determined in part by the broader movements of the nation as a whole. While we do not wish to negate the role of threshold changes unanticipated by either of these factors, the examination of the past, particularly when it is addressed in the context of the national experience, should provide a baseline reference framework for the future.

Historical Population Change: 1960 to 1970

The patterns of the recent past are reviewed in Exhibit 1 which details New York City's population by age category from 1960 to 1970. While the overall population of the city increased slightly over the decade, each of the age-specific subsectors tended to show marked variations. For example, the number of children

EXHIBIT 4-1
NEW YORK CITY POPULATION CHANGE, BY AGE AND COLOR: 1960 TO 1970

Age Category	April 1, 1960	April 1, 1970	Change 1960-1970 Number	Change 1960-1970 Percent
		TOTAL		
TOTAL	7,781,984	7,894,862	112,878	1.5%
< 5	686,717	615,831	-70,886	-10.3
5-14	1,171,168	1,255,914	84,746	7.2
15-24	969,373	1,251,967	282,594	29.2
25-34	1,056,398	1,075,586	19,188	1.8
35-44	1,071,347	915,635	-155,712	-14.5
45-54	1,084,836	942,016	-142,820	-13.2
55-64	928,318	890,035	-38,283	-4.1
65+	813,827	947,878	134,051	16.5
		WHITE		
TOTAL	6,640,662	6,048,841	-591,821	-8.9%
< 5	546,341	422,343	-123,998	-22.7
5-14	961,387	855,860	-105,527	-11.0
15-24	818,486	935,875	117,389	14.3
25-34	866,703	784,015	-82,688	-9.5
35-44	888,578	677,320	-211,258	-23.8
45-54	955,613	755,111	-200,502	-21.0
55-64	844,155	769,057	-75,098	-8.9
65+	759,399	849,260	89,861	11.8
		NONWHITE		
TOTAL	1,141,322	1,846,021	704,699	61.7%
< 5	140,376	193,488	53,112	37.8
5-14	209,781	400,054	190,273	90.7
15-24	150,887	316,092	165,205	109.5
25-34	189,695	291,571	101,876	53.7
35-44	182,769	238,315	55,546	30.4
45-54	129,223	186,905	57,682	44.6
55-64	84,163	120,978	36,815	43.7
65+	54,428	98,618	44,190	81.2

Source: U.S. Bureau of the Census.

under the age of five declined by 70,886, or 10.3 percent; exhibiting even greater rates and absolute magnitudes of decline were the 35-to 44-(-14.5 percent or
155,712 people) and 45-to 54-(-13.2 percent or 142,820
people) years-of-age categories, the latter encompassing those New York City residents at the prime center
of the labor force. The 55-to 64-years-of-age group
also experienced shrinkage, but to a considerably lesser
extent (-4.1 percent). Consequently, the city lost
336,000 people over the age of 35.

Offsetting this decline were two disparate growth
sectors. The first is contained within the relatively
youthful age span of 5 to 34 years. The bulk of the
increase (282,594 or 29.2 percent) was experienced in
the 15-to 24-years-of-age category which implies the
entrance of many young newcomers to the labor force with
concomitant pressures on the city's economic base. Of
equal relevance to the present (1977) in regards to the
latter concern is the 5 to 14 year-old age group, which
increased by 84,746 or 7.2 percent. As we shall note
later in more detail, much of the city's current unemployment pressures stems from this demographic reality -
the maturation of the products of the post-World War II
baby boom.

Distinct from these relatively youthful sectors
is the group of individuals 65 years of age and over,
whose growth increment totaled 134,051 (16.5 percent).
For every six persons in New York City over 65 in 1960,
there were seven by 1970. The significance of this
development for social service requirements, specialized
housing services, and related concerns is evident.

The variations discussed above - the patterns of
growth and decline across the age spectrum - are the surface reality masking equally significant but varied
undercurrents. To elaborate these phenomena, it is
necessary to refine the data partitions - to disassemble
the population matrix into white and nonwhite components.
The results of this disaggregation are presented in
the latter portions of Exhibit 1, maintaining the same
age breakdowns as the earlier part of the Exhibit. In
the context of a decade of minimal total city growth,
the nonwhite populace overall demonstrated a rate of
increase of 61.7 percent,increasing its proportional
share of the city's total population from 14.7 percent
to 28.4 percent. While positive growth increments were
experienced in every age category, they were most
dominant in the 5-to 14-and 15-to 24-years-of-age sectors. Again, the problems of nonwhite adolescent unemployment and the social trauma that stems from it

become much more understandable if viewed in terms of
age cohorts growing within a city whose capacity to
absorb entrants into the labor force has sadly diminished
over time. Absent migration, for example, the 400,054
nonwhite children aged 5 to 14 years in 1970 will - as
the latter stages of the 1970s decade approach - represent a very significant surge in newcomers to the labor
force.

It is also important to note at this juncture the
comparative youthfulness of New York City's nonwhite
population, particularly when contrasted with the white
population. For example, within the nonwhite sector,
there were twice as many children under the age of 5
as individuals over the age of 65. The same comparison
within the white population was inverted, with only half
as many children under the age of 5 as individuals over
the age of 65. Therefore, just as a consequence of the
natural aging of the population, all other factors
held constant, the relative ratio of whites and nonwhites in the city would shift quite markedly.

But the data presented above provide yet additional
insights into the dynamics that are at work. While the
nonwhite population was growing at a rate of almost 62
percent over the 1960 to 1970 period, the total white
population declined by 8.9 percent. For the most part,
the pattern of white population decline both mirrors and
underpins that evidenced by the total city population.
There were only two white age sectors that demonstrated
growth: the baby boom offspring, those 15 to 24 years
of age, which increased by 14.3 percent; and the elderly,
those 65 years old and over, whose numbers increased by
11.8 percent. The largest decreases were recorded in
the age spans of 35 to 54 years and under 5 years. It
is important to note that the scale of decline of the
former group (aged 35 to 54 years) - encompassing those
individuals typically at or near the peak of their earning capacity - was greater than 400,000. The growth of
the nonwhite age equivalent compensated for only one
quarter of this total loss.

Migration: 1960 to 1970

The data presented in Exhibit 1 summarize but cloak
the extraordinarily complex process of population change,
the two basic components of which are migration and net
natural increase. Migration is of enormous significance,
not only serving to differentiate between the city's
basic demographics and those of the nation, but also
giving insight into the residential decisionmaking

process. The latter, in turn, tends to reflect whether
the city's offerings - economic, cultural, or any of
the other elements that constitute residential appeal -
have been found wanting. Therefore, detailing migration by age and color for the 1960 to 1970 period becomes
essential for evaluating the longitudinal dimension of
population change (see Exhibit 2).

Over the ten-year time span, the total net outmigration (outmovers minus inmovers) for the city approached
the 500,000 person level. However, this was the aggregate result of the net outmigration of 882,516 whites
and the positive inflow of 385,233 nonwhites. Therefore,
a number of distinct processes underlie the overall city
migration experinece. It is possible to infer the outlines of these dynamics by scrutinizing the unique age
profiles of the two mover groups. Within the white
population emerges the picture of a vast outmigration
of relatively youthful families, gauged by the net
residual of 171,633 whites in the 35 to 44 years of age
bracket who vacated the city, complemented by a net outflow of 324,751 children under the age of 14. Thus the
momentum of the white outmigration appeared to have been
spearheaded by households in the child-rearing stage of
the family life cycle.

In addition, two other white subsets can be suggested. First, a large component of outmigration comprised the white elderly (65 years of age and over) -
with 170,639 (net) leaving New York despite the absolute
growth of this group as a whole over the course of the
decade (see Exhibit 1). At least in part this may have
been a reflection of the pulling power of the Sunbelt,
luring those elderly who have the fiscal and physical
capacity to take advantage of balmier climates.

The second subset of note is the small net outmigration in the 15-to 34-years-of-age group. If the age profile is refined to five-year intervals (the level of
detail operationalized in the projection methodology),
it is possible to uncover several positive migration
components. These are isolated in the note to Exhibit
2; despite net white migration losses in every gross
ten-year classification interval, there were select male
(25 to 29 years) and female (20 to 29 years) sectors to
whom the city may still have represented a positive lure.
These were, most likely, young professional individuals
not in the process of childbearing.

In contrast, all of the nonwhite age partitions
exhibited positive migration balances, with the dis-
tributional pattern indicating a substantial influx of

EXHIBIT 4-2
NEW YORK CITY MIGRATION TOTALS,
BY AGE AND COLOR: 1960 TO 1970

Age Category	Total	White	Nonwhite
TOTAL	-497,283	-882,516	385,233
< 5	- 57,894	- 65,820	7,926
5-14	-185,795	-258,931	73,136
15-24	81,932	- 16,350	98,282
25-34	116,183	- 15,751	131,934
35-44	-124,226	-171,633.	47,407
45-54	- 72,857	- 90,136	17,279
55-64	- 86,478	- 93,256	6,778
65+	-168,148	-170,639	2,491

Note: When disaggregated by five-year intervals and by sex, the white population does exhibit positive migration components.

	15-19	20-24	25-29	30-34
White Female	-15,372	35,382	16,800	-39,562
White Male	-25,638	-10,722	20,989	-13,978

Source: Gladys K. Bowles, Calvin L. Beale, and Everett S. Lee, Net Migration of the Population, 1960-1970 by Age, Sex, and Color, Part I - Northeastern States and Counties (Athens, Georgia: Economic Research Service, U.S. Department of Agriculture; The Institute for Behavioral Research, University of Georgia; Applied Research to National Needs, National Science Foundation, 1975.)

relatively youthful individuals to the city. Of the
total net nonwhite inmigration (385,233 individuals),
less than 7 percent (26,548) were 45 years of age and
over - beyond the childbearing years. The vast bulk
of the inmigrants (303,532) - over three out of four -
were in the 5 to 34 years of age bracket.

The Components of Change: 1960 to 1970

Exhibit 3 completes the summary of the city's 1960
to 1970 population change by placing migration in the
context of net natural increase - the natural aging (or
survival) of the base population, including births.
(The total net natural increase is equivalent to births
minus deaths.) For the population as a whole, migration,
while of considerable magnitude (-497,283 people) was
more offset by a net natural increase of 610,161 individuals. However, to amplify the significance of these
components for future changes in New York City's population, a comparison between the white and nonwhite sectors
again proves useful. For the former, the 882,516 net
outmigrants far outweighed the population gains through
net natural increase (290,695 people). In contrast, the
nonwhite population, whose magnitude was only 17.2 percent that of whites in 1960 and 30.5 percent in 1970, had
a larger net natural increase over the intervening period
(319,466).

The age-specific patterns within each of these subsets appear to diverge markedly, but many similarities are
apparent. For example, the cohorts encompassing the low
birth rates of the Depression and World War II were abnormally small and, as they aged, they replaced cohorts
of larger magnitude. By 1970, they had entered into
the 25-to 34-and 35-to 44-years-of-age categories, both
of which registered declines for the white population.
For the nonwhite equivalents, the former age group (25
to 34 years) showed the only net natural decrease within
the nonwhite profile, while the latter group (35 to 44)
had the smallest positive increase.

Similarly the largest net natural increases for
both subsets (excluding the white elderly) occurred in
the age groups spanning 5 to 24 years, into which the
abnormally large postwar baby boom cohorts had matured
by 1970. Broad historical events, then, weigh heavily
in the overall process of population change, and are
altered only by the realities of migration.

EXHIBIT 4-3
NEW YORK CITY, COMPONENTS OF POPULATION CHANGE, BY AGE AND COLOR: 1960 TO 1970

Age Category	Population Change	Migration	Net Natural Increase
TOTAL			
TOTAL	112,878	-497,283	610,161
< 5	-70,886	- 57,894	-12,992
5-14	84,746	-185,795	270,541
15-24	282,594	81,932	200,662
25-34	19,188	116,183	-96,995
35-44	-155,712	-124,226	-31,486
45-54	-142,820	- 72,857	-69.963
55-64	- 38,283	- 86,478	48,195
65+	134,051	-168,148	302,199
WHITE			
TOTAL	-591,821	-882,516	290,695
< 5	-123,998	- 65,820	- 58,178
5-14	-105,527	-258,931	153,404
15-24	117,389	- 16,350	133,739
25-34	- 82,688	- 15,751	- 66,937
35-44	-211,258	-171,633	- 39,625
45-54	-200,502	- 90,136	-110,366
55-64	- 75,098	- 93,256	18,158
65+	89,861	-170,639	260,500
NONWHITE			
TOTAL	704,699	385,233	319,466
< 5	53,112	7,926	45,186
5-14	190,273	73,136	117,137
15-24	165,205	98,282	66,923
25-34	101,876	131,934	-30,058
35-44	55,546	47,407	8,139
45-54	57,682	17,279	40,403
55-64	36,815	6,778	30,037
65+	44,190	2,491	41,699

Source: U.S. Bureau of the Census.
Gladys K. Bowles, Calvin L. Beale, and Everett S. Lee, Net Migration of the Population, 1960-1970 by Age, Sex, and Color, Part I - Northeastern States and Counties (Athens, Georgia: Economic Research Service, U.S. Department of Agriculture; The Institute for Behavioral Research, University of Georgia; Applied Research to National Needs, National Science Foundation, 1975.)

Despite the white-nonwhite similarities and their
underlying causal rationale, some variations do exist.
The most prominent is the net natural decrease of
58,178 children under the age of 5 within the white
population, while the nonwhite population demonstrated a
positive increment (45,186) for the equivalent age sector. As will be noted in more detail subsequently,
this incongruity is a result of the variation not only
in the fertility rates but also in the relative proportion of each population subset in the childbearing
age ranges.

Age Structure Patterns: New York City
Versus the United States

The broader historical patterns are national in
scope, and are not unique to New York City. By using
the corresponding age distributions within the United States
as a comparative baseline, both the general and unique attributes of New York City's population distribution are
exposed. In 1960, for example, New York City's age profile
was similar in general to that of the nation (see Exhibit
4). However, the city did exhibit a skew toward a more
elderly population. In the categories above and below 35
years of age, the city tended to be over- and underrepresented, respectively, with the largest discrepancies in
the 55-to 64-and 5-to 14-years-of-age sectors.

By 1970 (Exhibit 5), despite the fact that the nation's
total growth rate (13.3 percent) far exceeded that of New
York (1.5 percent), the evolving age profiles tended to
maintain a considerable degree of correspondence. Particularly significant indicators in this regard are the percentage changes presented at the bottom of Exhibit 5.
While differences in magnitude were evident, the directional patterns of change were remarkedly congruent.
In both the national and local contexts, the surging baby
boom cohort (15-to 24-years-of-age) and the receding
baby bust generation (less than 5 years of age) clearly
emerged. Significantly, the shrinkage within the older
age spans (35 to 64 years of age) in New York resulted
in the convergence of the local-national age structures.

SUMMARY

The 1960 to 1970 period is the last time interval
fully covered by the decennial census enumerations.
Since comparable data accounts will not become available until the early 1980s, and since the patterns

EXHIBIT 4-4
AGE STRUCTURE PATTERNS
NEW YORK CITY AND THE UNITED STATES: APRIL 1, 1960
(Numbers in thousands)

	Total	*< 5*	*5–14*	*15–24*	*25–34*	*35–44*	*45–54*	*55–64*	*65+*
						AGE CATEGORY			
United States	179,323	20,321	35,465	24,020	22,818	24,081	20,485	15,572	16,560
New York City	7,782	687	1,171	969	1,056	1,071	1,085	928	814
			PERCENT DISTRIBUTION						
United States	100.0	11.3	19.8	13.4	12.7	13.4	11.4	8.7	9.2
New York City	100.0	8.8	15.0	12.5	13.6	13.8	13.9	11.9	10.5

Source: U.S. Bureau of the Census.

EXHIBIT 4-5
AGE STRUCTURE PATTERNS
NEW YORK CITY AND THE UNITED STATES: APRIL 1, 1970
(Numbers in thousands)

	Total	< 5	5-14	15-24	25-34	35-44	45-54	55-64	65+
				AGE CATEGORY					
United States	203,212	17,154	40,746	35,441	24,907	23,088	23,220	18,590	20,066
New York City	7,895	616	1,256	1,252	1,076	916	942	890	948
			PERCENT DISTRIBUTION						
United States	100.0	8.4	20.1	17.4	12.3	11.4	11.4	9.1	9.9
New York City	100.0	7.8	15.9	15.9	13.6	11.6	11.9	11.3	12.0
			PERCENT CHANGE: 1960 TO 1970						
United States	13.3	-15.6	14.9	47.5	9.2	-4.1	13.4	19.4	21.2
New York City	1.5	-10.3	7.3	29.2	1.9	-14.5	-13.2	-4.1	16.5

Source: U.S. Bureau of the Census.

documented over the period carry substantial historical
inertia, their isolation and review is a mandatory preliminary to effective evaluation of the projection results.

1. *While the population of the United States
   increased by 13.3 percent from 1960 to 1970,
   that of New York increased by 1.5 percent.
   The city's white population declined by 8.9
   percent (591,821 people), but was compensated
   by a nonwhite increase of 61.7 percent (704,699).*

2. *The only white age groups within the city to
   show positive gains were the 15-to 24-years-of
   age group (into which the baby boom cohort had
   aged by 1970) and the elderly, those 65 years
   of age and over. The nonwhite population demonstrated increases throughout the age continuum,
   but the gains were greater in the more youthful
   age sectors.*

3. *The major components of poulation change comprise migration and net natural increase. Although New York City had a net outmigration of
   497,283 individuals, the net natural increase
   (610,161) was sufficient for the city to register a population increase in total.*

4. *The migrational experience was dominated by the
   following patterns:*

   a. *The overall city migration total was
      a consequence of a white net outmigra-
      tion of 882,516 people and a nonwhite
      net inmigration of 385,233 people.*

   b. *The white outmigration cut across all
      of its component age sectors (when
      defined by ten year intervals). However,
      the major losses encompassed those age
      groups which can be inferred to re-
      present households in the childrearing
      stage of the family life cycle, as well
      as the elderly (65 years of age and
      over). However, further age and sex
      disaggregations did reveal the presence
      of positive migration segments--young
      individuals in their 20s probably not
      in the process of childrearing.*

   c. *The vacating of the city by white family-
      raising households was paralleled by*

*the inmigration of their nonwhite counter-
parts. The latter represented a major
proportion of a positive nonwhite migration flow which was characteristic of
all its age groups.*

5. *The city's net natural increase - the consequence
of births in conjunction with the aging of its
base population - reflected both broader national
trends and the age structure of the population
of the base period.*

   a. *The pattern of white net natural increase
   exactly paralleled that of the city as a
   whole. Declines were evident in the age
   groups under 5 years and between 25 and
   54 years of age. The latter was a consequence of the low birth rates of the
   Depression and World War II era, as well
   as the aging of those cohorts depleted
   by the earlier suburbanization flows of
   the 1950 to 1960 period. Positive increases were registered in the ranks of
   the elderly and those age sectors into
   which the baby boom bulge had aged.*

   b. *The nonwhite population exhibited sharp
   gains through the process of net natural
   increase in all age sectors except in
   the 25-to 34-year-old group (which declined) and the 35-to 44 year-old group
   (which showed a minimal gain). Again,
   in 1970 these age ranges reflected the
   historic birth rate declines of the
   1930s and early 1940s.*

6. *The overall age structure changes within New York
City generally mirrored those changes taking
place at the national scale. As we look to the
future, then, the national trendline is a factor
of overriding concern. It is to this subject
that attention is now directed.*

AN OVERVIEW

Before presenting the detailed city population projection results, it is useful to undertake a broad overview of the population changes anticipated for the nation
as a whole for the corresponding time intervals. A second
preliminary evaluation is then provided - a brief

comparison between the national trendlines and those
forecast for New York City. While it may be considered premature to present such an analysis before the
projection results are examined in detail, this preliminary overview should prove an important adjunct to
the latter task. What will become particularly evident
is the degree to which the New York City experience is
linked to the national dynamic, while also reflecting
its unique historical attributes as well as its distinct migrational patterns.

The National Age Structure Evolution

There are three major age structural patterns that
have dominated the nation's population shifts during
the last 25 years and whose implications will be basic
to the future: the baby boom, the baby bust, and the
growth of the elderly population. These patterns have
been and will be reflected in New York City, whatever
unique elements are present. The post-World War II
baby boom, the first phenomenon, was initiated in 1946
by an approximate 20 percent increase in the number of
live births compared to that recorded in 1945. A steady
increase in the annual number of births continued to
1957, the peak year of the postwar era, generating about
47 million children over this twelve-year span.[3] This
group has inserted a permanent but moving bulge into
America's age structure, flooding the nation's school
systems in the 1950s and 1960s, its higher educational
systems in the 1960s and 1970s, and its job and housing
markets in the 1970s.

The subsequent baby bust, etched deeply into the
nation's population ledgers, is foreordained to trail
the wake of the baby boom tide as it matures through
the country's age structure. While the baby boom produced
47 million children during the twelve-year period from
1946 to 1957, the number of live births in the last
twelve-year period, 1965 to 1976, was only 41 million,
accentuating the sheer size of the predecessor cohorts.[4]
Facilities and opportunities predicated on the baby
boom are and will be experiencing the effects of a
shrinking clientele. At the same time, the unique strains
caused by the baby boom at each stage of its maturation
may be mitigated over time by the reduced scale of the
trailing "baby bust" cohorts.

Finally, the elderly - those 65 years of age and
over - are continually increasing in number and significance. In total they have virtually doubled to 23

million people over the last two and one-half decades,
and now account (1976) for almost 11 percent of the
nation's population (as compared to 8.1 percent in 1950).[5]

The overall age structural evolution encompassing
these three developments has profound reverberations to
which no national subarea is immune. In the following
analysis, national shifts will be reviewed so as to provide a reference framework for evaluating the projected
structure and composition of the city's population over
the next decade. Since the rate of fertility is an important determinant of these trendlines, a brief review
of its recent history is useful.

Fertility Rates

Exhibit 6 presents one of the key demographic variables, indicating the trends in fertility over the past
two and one-half decades.[6] In the 1950 to 1954 period,
the total rate was at the 3.337 level, i.e., 3,337
children were born per 1,000 women. The peak in modern
times was experienced in the 1955 to 1959 period when
the total rate increased to 3.690. Since that time,
however, it has decreased very sharply, with the 1970
to 1974 average fertility rate standing at 2.106, a
level just below the replacement threshold. (As a point
of reference, a total fertility rate of 2.115 represents
"replacement level" fertility for the total population
under current mortality conditions.)

Just how precipitous this decline has been is revealed in the latter half of Exhibit 6, where the rate
attendant to each individual year of the 1970s is presented. There is a steady decline in each of these
benchmarks. Indeed, the 1.760 rate of 1976 is 29 percent less than the 2.480 rate of 1970, almost 17 percent
below the replacement level rate.

This does not mean, however, that the population of
the United States, even without immigration, faces im-
minent decline; given the increasing number of women of
childbearing age, the immediate prospect is for sustained
net natural increases (births minus deaths) in the nation's
total population. To highlight this situation, a summary
of the detailed components of population change is
necessary.

EXHIBIT 4-6
TOTAL UNITED STATES FERTILITY RATE:
1950 TO 1974 BY FIVE YEAR PERIODS
AND 1970 TO 1976 BY YEAR

Period	Rate
1950-1954	3.337
1955-1959	3.690
1960-1964	3.459
1965-1969	2.636
1970-1974	2.106

Year	
1970	2.480
1971	2.275
1972	2.022
1973	1.896
1974	1.857
1975	1.799
1976	1.760

Note: The fertility rate indicates how many births a woman would have by the end of her child-bearing years if, during her entire reproductive period, she were to experience the age-specific birth rates for the given period.

Source: U.S. Bureau of the Census, Current Population Reports, Series P-20, No. 307, "Population Profile of the United States: 1976," U.S. Government Printing Office, Washington, D.C., April 1977.

The Components of Population Change

As shown in Exhibit 7, given the continual decrease
in the fertility rate over the 1970 to 1976 period, the
net natural increase declined from 1.8 million people in
1970 to below 1.2 million people in 1973, then proceeded
to rise very slowly above the 1.2 million person plateau
between 1973 and 1976. The same pattern is evident in
the total number of births, with an apparent bottoming
out in 1973. These slight upward shifts are a consequence of the changing age structure of the United States,
as will be detailed subsequently. Nonetheless, the
significance of the low number of births in 1976 (3.163
million) is emphasized by the magnitude of those recorded
at the 1957 peak (4.308 million); over 1.1 million more
births occurred in 1957 than in 1976.[7]

At the same time, with the exception of the unique
Vietnamese incursion of 1975, net civilian immigration
has tended to shrink over time, declining from 438,000 in
1970 to 314,000 in 1976. Unfortunately, the changing
dimensions of illegal immigration into the United States
are not captured by the standard data accounts, and are
not part of any succeeding analysis.

The Future

Variations in the future will continue to be a function of the fertility rate and the number of women of
childbearing age, assuming that mortality rates and immigration levels do not change significantly. As will be
explored subsequently, the number of women of childbearing age will be increasing significantly over the
next decade - the products of the maturation of the post-
World War II baby boom - making it possible for the number
of births to increase even in the context of reduced
fertility. Additionally, the sheer size of the fertile
cohorts could amplify any positive fertility rate fluctuations into much larger population growth consequences.

The Census Bureau's most recent projections comprise three different series, each reflecting different
assumptions about the rate of fertility. In Exhibit 8,
the Series III projection, which assumes a fertility rate
moving toward the 1.700 level, is employed. Additionally,
it assumes a slight improvement in mortality and an annual net immigration of 400,000 people. In the analysis
which follows, the actual experience for the years between 1970 and 1975 has been recorded.

EXHIBIT 4-7

ESTIMATES OF THE COMPONENTS OF POPULATION CHANGE FOR THE UNITED STATES, JANUARY 1, 1970 TO JANUARY 1, 1977

(Numbers in thousands)

Year	Population at Beginning of Period [1]	Total Increase [2]	Natural Increase			Net Civilian Immigration
			Net	Births	Deaths	
1970	203,849	2,227	1,812	3,739	1,927	438
1971	206,076	2,012	1,626	3,556	1,930	387
1972	208,088	1,623	1,293	3,258	1,965	325
1973	209,711	1,496	1,163	3,137	1,974	331
1974	211,207	1,541	1,225	3,160	1,935	316[3]
1975	212,748	1,687	1,238	3,149	1,911	450[3]
1976	214,435	1,563	1,249	3,163	1,914	314
1977	215,118	-	-	-	-	-

Notes:
1. Total population, including Armed Forces overseas.
2. Includes estimates of overseas admissions into and discharges from the Armed Forces and for 1970, includes error of closure between censuses.
3. Includes about 130,000 Vietnamese refugees who entered the United States during 1975.

Source: U.S. Bureau of the Census, Current Population Reports, Series P-20, No. 307, "Population Profile of the United States: 1976," U.S. Government Printing Office, Washington, D.C., April 1977.

The 1970 to 1975 Period

In the 1970 to 1975 period, the aging products of the baby boom dominated the total national growth increment - almost 60 percent (6 million people) of the nation's 1970 to 1975 total growth (10.3 million people) were between the ages of 25 to 34 years, the period of household formation and peak childbearing (see Exhibit 8). Similarly. the 15-to 24-years-of-age sector, the period of labor-force entry, also continued to expand (by 4.8 million people) but at a rate lesser than that of the previous ten years (see Exhibit 5).

Despite the burgeoning of these fertile sectors of society, declining birth rates resulted in a 1.3 million person contraction in the under-five-years-of-age group. The decline of the latter experienced during the preceding decade now impacted the 5-to 14-years-of-age group, which receded by 3 million people from 1970 to 1975.

The accession rate to the ranks of the elderly expanded markedly, and given the declining number of births, the elderly constituted almost 28 percent of the national growth increment.

At mid-decade, then, the population outlines of the short-term future have started to come into focus. The baby boom offspring are in their childbearing and household formation years and are exerting pressures on the American economy to produce jobs for an unprecedented number of young adults. Similarly, this 25-to 34-years-of-age cluster implies a major growth sector for the housing market. It is this major evolution that has influenced New York City in the past five years and will prove significant in the future. And, in the context of the decline in the number of children under five years of age, the locational choices of these individuals may not be constrained to suburban "childbearing" environments as they were in the preceeding two decades.

The Immediate Future: 1975 to 1980

It should be pointed out that for 1980 and 1985 the projections for the older groups are independent of the birth rate - the individuals are already alive and the total numbers in their respective age cohorts are reasonably assured, at least to the degree the mortality rate and immigration assumptions are valid.

EXHIBIT 4-8
UNITED STATES POPULATION CHANGE, BY AGE: 1970 TO 1985

	April 1, 1970	Change: 1970-1975	July 1, 1975	Change: 1975-1980	July 1, 1980	Change: 1980-1985	July 1, 1985
TOTAL	203,212	10,328	213,540	7,192	220,732	8,147	228,879
< 5	17,154	-1,272	15,882	-1,289	14,593	1,642	16,235
5-14	40,746	-3,012	37,734	-3,838	33,896	-2,502	31,394
15-24	35,441	4,803	40,244	1,283	41,527	-3,010	38,517
25-34	24,907	6,011	30,918	5,254	36,172	3,687	39,859
35-44	23,086	- 273	22,815	2,906	25,721	5,655	31,376
45-54	23,220	548	23,768	-1,070	22,698	-241	22,457
55-64	18,590	1,184	19,774	1,424	21,198	539	21,737
65+	20,066	2,339	22,405	2,522	24,927	2,378	27,305

Source: U.S. Bureau of the Census, Current Population Reports, Series P-25, No. 704, "Projections of the Population of the United States: 1977 to 2050," U.S. Government Printing Office, Washington, D.C., 1977.

The maturing residuals of the boom-bust cycle continue to dominate the age-structure changes - the bulk
of the baby boom bulge will have aged to between 25
and 34 years of age by 1980. Indeed, the 5.3 million
person increase in this age sector will account for
73 percent of the national growth increment between 1975
and 1980 (see Exhibit 8).

Virtually countering this expansion will be the
sharp contraction of the under-14-years-of-age group by
approximately 5.1 million people; the baby bust, then,
will finally be impacting American society in full force.
Between 1970 and 1980, it is probable that the school
age population will decline by over 6.8 million people,
fostering significant adjustments for educational and
child-related institutions and services.[8] Indeed, the
school budget and school bond issues of yesteryear are
giving way to the school closing issues of today and to-
morrow.

The prime executive cum technical and vocational
age group, 35 to 44 years of age, is expected to expand
substantially, increasing by more than 2.9 million people
in the 1975 to 1980 period. While this will be partially
offset by a decline of 1.1 million persons in the 45-
to 54-years-of-age group, the pressures for entrance
into the executive suite will continue. Once again, the
elderly will be a significant growth sector with a net
increase of 2.5 million people expected - or roughly
500,000 additional persons a year reaching the nominal
retirement age and surviving between 1975 and 1980.

The 1980 to 1985 Period

By 1985, America's population will have grown by
15.3 million people from its 1975 level. The great
baby boom bulge will by then have begun to enter the
35-to 44-years-of-age sector, which will expand by 3.7
million people. The elderly will continue to escalate
in number with a net addition of more than 2.4 million
individuals over the age of sixty-five.

Equally significant, however, is the maturation
of the baby bust cohort, which will clearly and specifically impact the nation's institutions of higher
learning. Those between the ages of 15 and 24 years
will decline by more than 3 million people. Corollary
to this impact will be the initial stages of a decline
in the number of newcomers to the job market.

When we compare the age structure profile of America's population in 1975 with that of 1985, the scale of the transformation becomes evident. There will be a growth of more than 4.9 million people over the age of 65, plus a net addition of almost 2.0 million people between 55 and 64 years of age. Subject to changes in social security and pension legislation, the number of those exiting from the labor force may be very significant indeed.

Related to this observation is the decline (1.3 million) in the 45-to 54-years-of-age category (the Depression era progeny) many of whom are in their peak earning years. Undoubtedly, much of the growth in the labor force will take place in the 25-to 34-and the 35-to 44 -years-of-age groups (the baby boom products), whose numbers will increase by 8.9 million and 8.6 million people respectively.

In contrast, the 15-to 24-years-of-age group will be in decline (-1.7 million people) as the initial segments of the baby bust reach adulthood, perhaps diminishing the number of entrants into the labor force. The main sag, however, will be experienced in the 5-to 14-years-of-age cohort, which will contract by 6.3 million individuals. To say that these declines will challenge the conventions and service infrastructures established throughout the decade of the 1960s is to state the obvious.

The Major Patterns

These, then, are the major age structural changes characterizing the evolution of America's population. To briefly summarize the major patterns, the following presentation delineates the primary and secondary age growth sectors (deleting the young and elderly extremes) for each of the time periods examined, including the 1960 to 1970 changes (with the numbers in parentheses indicating the rates of change):

Key Age Growth Sectors

	Primary	Secondary
1960 to 1970	15-24 (47.5%)	5-14 (14.9%)
1970 to 1975	25-34 (24.1%)	15-24 (13.6%)
1975 to 1980	25-34 (17.0%)	35-44 (12.7%)
1980 to 1985	35-44 (22.0%)	25-34 (10.2%)

These sectors document the historic and future episode of
the baby boom over a twenty-five-year period; from the
present time through 1985, they will successively swell
the 25-to 34-and 35 -to 44 -years-of -age groups.

At the same time, the national context reveals age
sectors of contracting magnitude, the residuals both of
history (the precipitors of decline in the Depression era
birthrate) and more recent social phenomenon (the baby
bust).

Age Decline Sectors

	Primary	Secondary
1960 to 1970	< 5 (-15.6%)	35-44 (-4.1%)
1970 to 1975	0--14 (- 7.4%)	35-44 (-1.2%)
1975 to 1980	0-14 (- 9.6%)	45-54 (-4.5%)
1980 to 1985	5-24 (- 7.3%)	45-54 (-1.1%)

These secular patterns set the stage for the population
events of national subareas; future discrepancies will be
a function of past deviations in age structure as well as
the variable impact of migration.

The National-New York City Comparison

Exhibit 9 compares the age sector growth rates of
New York City's population to those of the nation as a
whole for each of the major intervals between 1960 and
1985. Overall, the patterns of change tend to be similar,
at least in direction, with the historic 1960 to 1970
differentials maintained over time.

For the 1960 to 1970 period, already documented,
both sets of observations showed primary growth in the
15-to 24 -years-of-age groups, and secondary growth (ignoring the more mature segments of each population) in the
5 -to 14-years-of -age sectors. The major differences centered about the losses experienced in New York City's
45 -to 64-years-of-age category.

The estimates for the 1970 to 1975 period show
analogous patterns of similarity and divergence. While
the nation secured a 5.1 percent gain in population, the
city suffered a 5.1 percent decline. The primary and
secondary growth sectors of the nation - the 25-to 34-
and 15 -to 24 -years-of age groups, respectively - were
replicated within New York City. Additionally, both
registered rates of decline in the 14-years-of-age and
under category. However, the city's continued losses
in the 45 -years-and-over age group remained a distinct
phenomenon.

EXHIBIT 4-9
AGE STRUCTURE CHANGES: 1960 TO 1985
NEW YORK CITY AND THE UNITED STATES

	1960 to 1970		1970 to 1975	
	United States	New York City	United States	New York City
TOTAL	13.3	1.5	5.1	-5.1
< 5	-15.6	-10.3	-7.4	-19.3
5-14	14.9	7.3	-7.4	-17.1
15-24	47.5	29.2	13.6	3.5
25-34	9.2	1.9	24.1	25.3
35-44	-4.1	-14.5	-1.2	-15.7
45-54	13.4	-13.2	2.4	-10.8
55-64	19.4	-4.1	6.4	-13.3
65+	21.2	16.5	11.7	-2.4

	1975 to 1980		1980 to 1985	
	United States	New York City	United States	New York City
TOTAL	3.4	-1.3	3.7	-2.2
<5	-8.1	4.6	11.3	1.5
5-14	-10.2	-20.1	-7.4	-10.7
15-24	3.2	-1.7	-7.2	-15.0
25-34	17.0	16.3	10.2	3.3
35-44	12.7	13.5	22.0	32.8
45-54	04.5	-16.5	-1.1	-16.4
55-64	7.2	-9.5	2.5	-11.4
65+	11.3	-0.3	9.5	-3.6

Note: Percents computed from rounded data

Source: CUPR Projections; Exhibits 4,5, and 8.

In the 1975 to 1980 projection period, both the
nation and city exhibit virtually identical change in
the primary (25-to 34-years-of-age) and secondary (35-
to 44-years-of-age) growth sectors. Only the extremes
of the age continuum, under 5 years and 55 years of age
and over, show directional differences.

The final projection interval, 1980 to 1985, finds
the major growth sector moving into the 35-to 44-years-
of-age group for both New York City and the nation, with
secondary growth registered in the 25-to 34-years-of-age
category (ignoring the nation's under-5-years-of-age
sector which shows significant growth for the first time
since 1960). While the rates vary between the nation and
the city, the directional flows are similar except in
the 55-years-of-age and over categories.

The end result of this series of age-specific
changes is marked alterations in the age-structure profiles of New York City and the nation. These are presented in Exhibit 10, with the largest corresponding age
categories of the nation and city underlined. Despite
the shifts experienced in each profile set, the general
nature of the transformations is apparent - both clearly
reflect the baby boom (the shrinkage of the 5-to 14-
year-old category after 1970 and the contraction of the
15-to 24-year-old sector after 1975). Within this pattern, New York City is distinct in the marked concentration of its population in the 25-to 34-years-of-age
sector for 1975, 1980, and 1985.

The Working Age Population

One final note with regard to the national experience is warranted. The expected curtailment of the flow
of new entrants to the labor force during the 1980s has
been chronicled as foreshadowing an era of labor force
shortages. As the nation's and New York City's economies
struggle with the rapid ascension of large number of
individuals entering their working age years, some
degree of comfort is invoked over this impending development and there is a tendency to consider immediate
difficulties as being only short-term, due to fade as
the baby bust cohorts proceed to adulthood. Over the
next decade, however, the validity of such tentative
conventions may prove to be limited.

Certainly, the educational infrastructure dilemma
bespeaks of the effect wielded by shrinking age cohorts.
The impact in such instances is defined by the magnitude

EXHIBIT 4-10
AGE STRUCTURE PROFILES: 1960 TO 1985
NEW YORK CITY AND THE UNITED STATES

	1960	*1970*	*1975*	*1980*	*1985*
			NEW YORK CITY		
TOTAL	100.0	100.0	100.0	100.0	100.0
< 5	8.8	7.8	6.6	7.0	7.3
5-14	15.0	15.9	13.9	11.3	10.3
15-24	12.5	15.9	17.3	17.2	15.0
25-34	13.6	13.6	18.0	21.2	22.4
35-44	13.8	11.6	10.3	11.9	16.1
45-54	13.9	11.3	11.2	9.5	8.1
55-64	11.9	11.3	10.3	9.5	8.5
65+	10.5	12.0	12.3	12.5	12.3
			UNITED STATES		
TOTAL	100.0	100.0	100.0	100.0	100.0
< 5	11.3	8.4	7.4	6.6	7.1
5-14	19.8	20.1	17.7	15.4	13.7
15-24	13.4	17.4	18.8	18.8	16.8
25-34	12.7	12.3	14.5	16.4	17.4
35-44	13.4	11.4	10.7	11.7	13.7
45-54	11.4	11.4	11.1	10.3	9.8
55-64	8.7	9.1	9.3	9.6	9.5
65+	9.2	9.9	10.5	11.3	11.9

Source: See Exhibit 9.

of the immediately preceding age cohorts - the baby
boom generation supplanted by the trailing baby bust -
with the linkages and consequences immediate and apparent. However, the implications of this same phenomenon
for the labor force are not so easily specified. While
the number of entrants to the labor force over the 1980
to 1985 period may certainly be smaller than in the recent past (although changing labor force participation
rates may negate this assumption), the appropriate
evaluation may rest more in terms of those who are exiting
from the labor force at the opposite end of the age
spectrum. In 1980, for example (see Exhibit 8), there
are 33.9 million people aged 5 to 14 years. As they
age ten years, they will replace a population (15 to 24
years of age) whose size in 1980 is 41.5 million people,
indicating a perceptible decline in the number of labor
force entrants. Nonetheless, an equally telling comparison entails the 55-to 64-years-of-age sector, which in
1980 comprises 21.2 million individuals. For the moment
assuming these age groups adequately represent ingress
to and egress from the labor force, a cohort of 33.9
million people (5 to 14 years of age) will replace one
of 21.2 million people (55 to 64 years of age) over the
1980 to 1990 period, revealing overall growth of significant dimensions. While many aspects of this comparison
are inappropriate, it does provide some indication of
the size dimension attached to the labor force question.

    Assuming, for the purpose of simplicity, that the
15-to 64-years-of-age span is synonymous with both the
labor force and population of working age years, its
national pattern of growth is of the following format:

U.S. Population 15 to 64 Years of Age

1970	125.2 million
1975	137.5 million
1980	147.3 million
1985	153.9 million

While the magnitude of the increase does abate over the
1980 to 1985 period, the absolute gains are still considerable. (Indeed, if more precise labor force parameters were specified, taking into account changing
participation coefficients, the early 1980s experience
may well converge toward that of the late 1970s.) If
this eventuality permeates down to the scale of New
York City, even a stabilized local economy may not
prove sufficient to mitigate the city's unemployment
dilemmas. As will be presented in the following
chapter, it is this factor that adds impetus to outmigration and population decline.

Notes

1. For descriptions of the role of old-and new-law tenements in New York City's housing system, see: George Sternlieb and James W. Hughes, Housing and Economic Reality: New York City 1976 (New Brunswick, N.J.: Rutgers University, Center for Urban Policy Research, 1976), George Sternlieb and James W. Hughes, Housing and People in New York City (New York: Housing and Development Administration, 1973).

2. On July 1, 1945, the total population of the United States, including Armed Forces overseas, stood at 140.5 million people; by 1965, it broached the 194 million person level. U.S. Bureau of the Census, Current Population Reports, Series P-25, No. 704, "Projections of the Population of the United States: 1977 to 2050," U.S. Government Printing Office, Washington, D.C., 1977, p. 21.

3. U.S. Bureau of the Census, Current Population Reports, Series P-25, No. 706, "Estimates of the Population of the United States and Components of Change: 1940 to 1976," U.S. Government Printing Office, Washington, D.C., 1977, p.7.

4. Ibid.

5. U.S. Bureau of the Census, Current Population Reports, Series P-20, No. 307, "Population Profile of the United States: 1976," U.S. Government Printing Office, Washington, D.C., 1977, p. 12.

6. The total fertility rate for a given year shows how many births a group of 1000 women would have by the end of their childbearing years if, during their entire reproductive period, they were to experience the age-specific birth rates for the given year.

7. See source Note 3.

8. See: U.S. Bureau of the Census, Current Population Reports, Series P-20, No. 309, "School Enrollment-Social and Economic Characteristics of Students: October 1976," (Advance Report), U.S. Government Printing Office, Washington, D.C., 1977.

Chapter 5

NEW YORK CITY POPULATION PROJECTIONS

INTRODUCTION

Unobtrusively, but persistently, the post-1970 era has been permeated by profound sequences of metropolitan and regional change. As the more visible social turmoils of the previous decade have ebbed, they have been successively replaced by a gradual recognition of a long-term transformation of the nation's social and economic parameters. While very few changes have been manifested in explosive, media-attracting events, they are nonetheless promising to alter the national population contours on a heretofore unprecedented scale. While in many instances they raise significant questions about the continuity of past assumptions, they do not completely invalidate the secular momentum of past linkages.

For example, the emerging reference framework for interpreting urban decline has shifted from the older convention of urban-suburban competition (an intra-metropolitan framework) to much more complex notions of metropolitan-nonmetropolitan shifts (of people and jobs), interregional dynamics, and even international tensions.[1] Yet, whatever the scale of the causal nexus -- and the amplification of its area of impact -- it may not render obsolete the patterns of after-effect historically etched into the central city. Indeed, in large part, what appears to be occurring in the urban area is an acceleration of past trendlines and a reinforcement of the dynamics of change; their scope and magnitude may have been altered, but not their shape and pattern.

The New York City context may be prototypical of
the national phenomenon. In the first half of the decade of the 1970s, the nation's central cities, in total,
experienced for the first time absolute population losses, and these losses were substantial.[2] While this
appears to be a major shift in the historical trendline,
it is rather the elaboration of the traditional determinants of population change by the evolving regional
and metropolitan realities of the present decade. The
aging cities of the nation's industrial heartland - that
chain of massed human settlements forged in the industrial age, stretching from Boston to St. Louis - have
often recorded net migration losses (without experiencing actual population decline); these losses have suddenly increased in size and relative importance.

Underlying this development have been two major factors. The evolution and maturation of the nation's
economic system have as their geographic complement the
shift of economic activity to the southern rimlands at
the national scale - the Sunbelt - and to exurban-non-
metropolitan territories at the subregional level. The
conjunction of these shifts of economic activity with
the extant suburban movements has dramatically increased
and magnitude of the corrollary population flows, adding impetus to the migration of the more mobile population sectors of the central city.

Concurrently, the growth of migration takes on even
greater significance when coupled with the other major
component of population change - net natural increase.
In the past, the gains accrued by net natural increase
were sufficient to counter-balance and obscure both
the effects and the potency of the migrational dimension. Indeed, the rapid rates of national increase
characteristic of the postwar period into the 1960s
favored the existing distribution of the population -
the older settlements; they acted to confirm the vitality of established places by mitigating outmigration.
However, with the advent of a period of reduced fertility, migration's role in determining population change
has been thrust into increased importance and prominance
since net natural increases are no longer sufficient to
compensate for migrational attrition.

In keeping with this general pattern, New York City,
after a decade of virtual stability in size, was buf-
feted by sustained population losses in the immediate
post-1970 period, the corrollary to the erosion of its
economic base. And, given the assumptions and premises
of the projection model - high rates of outmigration

predicated on the continued depletion of the city's inventory of economic opportunities (jobs) and the persistence of low levels of net natural increase, the
best expectation for the 1975 to 1985 "post-crisis"
period is a continuation of recent events. But the
trend which initially surfaced in the 1970 to 1975
period should be considerably dampened in magnitude;
the severity of the absolute population losses should
abate appreciably. Nonetheless, the size and composition of the population of New York City circa 1985 will
stand in sharp contrast to that of 1970.

In the sections that follow, the analytical partitions established previously will be replicated. For
each of the benchmark years, the composition of the population will be defined by age and color disaggrega-
tions, with the intervening changes further elaborated
by migration and natural increase components. Before becoming enmeshed in the full intricacies of the presentations, it should prove useful to examine the broader
patterns of the anticipated developments.

THE BROADER PATTERNS OF CHANGE

The major components of the projected changes in
the pouplation of New York City are summarized in
Exhibit 1 for the three 5-year intervals between July
1, 1970 and July 1, 1985. As a point of reference, it
should be noted that between 1960 and 1970, the city
experience was one of minimal total growth - a net gain
of 112,878 residents was recorded over the intercensal
period. Between 1970 and 1975, however, a transformation of major proportions occurred; in this 5-year time
segment, it is estimated that the city's population
base eroded by 402,861 people or 5.1 percent, from
7,893,551 in 1970 to 7,490,690 in 1975. (The magnitude
and components of change for this period are in substantial agreement with those estimated by the U. S. Bureau
of the Census.)

This incipient decline foretells the dominant trendline for the ensuing ten years (1975 to 1985), the major
projection time frame. However, the declines should
abate, given their linkage to the patterns of economic
change (see Chapter 3). Between 1975 and 1980, for
example, the loss is projected to fall below the 100,000
person level (-99,180), less than 25 percent of the
decline registered for the previous five years. While the
early 1980s experience shows an increase in the magnitude
of decline (-160,312 people), the trauma of the early
1970s is far from replicated. Consequently, after the

EXHIBIT 5-1
COMPONENTS OF CHANGE 1970 TO 1985
NEW YORK CITY

1970 Population Base (April 1)	7,894,862	
1970 Population (July 1)	7,893,551	
1975 Population (July 1)	7,490,690	Change 1970 to 1975: -402,861
Survived 1970 Population	7,509,151	
Survived Births (1970 to 1975)	558,195 (12,436 deaths)	
Migration (1970 to 1975)	-576,656	
Net Natural Increase (Birth-Deaths)	173,795 (570,631-396,836)	
1980 Population (July 1)	7,391,510	Change 1975 to 1980: -99,180
Survived 1975 Population	7,189,634	
Survived Births (1975 to 1980)	568,258 (11,513 deaths)	
Migration (1975 to 1980)	-366,982	
Net Natural Increase (Births-Deaths)	267,802 (580,371-312,569)	

(continued)

EXHIBIT 5-1 (continued)
COMPONENTS OF CHANGE 1970 TO 1985
NEW YORK CITY

1985 Population   7,231,198   Change 1980 to 1985: -160,312

    Survived 1980
    Population   7,099,565

    Survived Births
    (1980 to 1985)   582,445 (11,077 deaths)

    Migration
    (1980 to 1985)   -450,812

    Net Natural
    Increase
    (Births-Deaths)   290,500 (593,522-393,022)

Source: CUPR Projections.

initiation of the decline phase during the 1970 to
1975 period, which buffetted the city with losses   exceeding 400,000 people, it appears that protracted but
slow erosion will define the New York City population
milieu, with an additional decline of almost 260,000
individuals anticipated for the ten years between 1975
and 1985. Contraction and shrinkage, then, will persist, notwithstanding their reduced scale.

The major dynamics of these projected changes center about the migration and net natural increase variables. (In Exhibit 1, the natural increase components
are a function of survived births and the difference
between the base year population and the survived base
year population.) Again as a point of reference, the
1960 to 1970 intercensal period revealed a net natural
increase of 610,161 people outweighing a net outmigration loss of -497,283 (see Exhibit 3). The relative
importance and magnitude of these parameters evolve
quite markedly in the 1970 to 1975 period. While it
is obvious that a major increase in outmigration
occurred (-576,656 from 1970 to 1975 versus -497,283
from 1960 to 1970), its significance is greatly en-
hanced by the diminished level of net natural increase
(173,795 versus 610,161), again acknowledging the
disparate time spans.

The effect of a doubling of the rate of outmigration has enormous consequences in and of itself. Moreover, when coupled with a virtual halving of the rate
of net natural increase, far greater changes are preci-
pitated in the absolute level of the population. This
is not unique to New York. The impetus given to outmigration by economic contraction in the nation's former centerpieces of industrial urbanization is accentuated by the declining role of net natural increase in
overall population change.

In the 1975 to 1980 projection interval, a perceptible abatement of the latter tendency is revealed.
As will be examined in more detail subsequently, the
increasing weight of the nonwhite population - which is
characterized by a younger age profile (with greater
survival rates) and somewhat higher levels of fertility
- tends to initiate a period of growth for the net
natural increase component in New York City (from
173,795 over the 1970 to 1975 period to 267,802 between
1975 and 1980). Nonetheless, even in the context of
reduced net outmigration (-366,982 individuals), a
consequence of diminished job losses, net natural increase is still insufficient to prohibit a continued

decline in the absolute level of the city's population
(-99,180 people). Yet the latter is appreciably smaller
than that of the preceding time interval (-402,861).

The 1980 to 1985 period shows the intractable nature
of the forces chronicled by the events of the 1970s decade. The net outmigrational component experiences an
upswing to over 450,000 people, a consequence not only
of the gradual attrition of the city's employment base
but also of the expansion of the labor force in excess
of the economy's ability to absorb it. As a result,
the city is projected to lose a total of 160,312 residents, despite continued gains in the natural increase
component (which will exceed 290,500 people).

So between 1970 and 1985, subject to the assumptions and premises of the projection methodology, New
York City's population will begin to approach the 7
million person plateau, in effect losing over 662,000
citizens. And, in what appears to be a secular transition - a reduced functional role as a residential and
economic nexus - net outmigration could approach 1.4
million people. Yet, even while these parameters of
change appear profound, their full complexity is understated at this level of analysis. Only when the more
detailed presentations are reviewed is the full import
of the city's evolution revealed. It is to this task
we now turn.

THE 1970 TO 1975 PERIOD

It has been five decades since New York City has
experienced a change in population size of the magnitude estimated for the 1970 to 1975 period. One has
to return to the 1920s - perhaps the pinnacle years of
the nation's foremost industrial metropolis, when the
city's fortunes were ascending rapidly - to find a five-
year period wherin the level of population shifted by
more than 400,000 people. However, in the earlier
period, the change was one of rapid expansion; in the
latter, it was one of abrupt contraction. In the
interim, the dual forces of industrial centralization
and urban growth have long since been transcended by
the post-industrial realities of decentralization and
urban shrinkage.

Emerging as if a belated recognition of this
broader national transformation - recorded only after
the fiscal crisis reached full force, *the city's popula-*
tion loss for the 1970 to 1975 period totaled 402,861
people (see Exhibit 2). (We have used the term "recorded" here with little hesitance, because of the correlation of this figure with the Census Bureau's estimates,
as noted earlier.) The overall decline, however, masks
substantial internal patterns of variation. Revealed
by the age distribution of the overall populace, the
losses exhibited a bimodal structure, heavily concentrated both in the more youthful sectors (14 years of
age and younger) and in the more mature age sectors
(35 years of age and over) of the city. Significantly,
the population whose ages span between 15 and 34 years
showed considerable growth, with the postwar baby boom
providing the growth impetus despite the overall am-
bience of decline.

The implications of this age transformation are
significant. On one hand, the city's educational infrastructure will certainly experience a diminishing level
of clientele; and, as will be evident below, its white/
nonwhite compositional changes may tax even further the
difficulties of adjustment. On the other hand, the requirements for labor force participation by the young
will provide an equally difficult challenge. As vexing
as the problems induced by overall population decline
are those manifested in evolving age structures.

Within this overall context, there are equally
striking white/nonwhite population transitions. *The*
projections indicate a decline of over 900,000 whites
in the city - approximately half of them concentrated
in the age groups under 14 years, with the bulk of the
remainder over 35 years old. Indeed, the only white
age sector demonstrating growth over this five-year
period was the 25-to 34-years-of-age group, the lingering reverberation of the baby boom. This appears to be
a key subpopulation relative to the demand for housing
and may account for part of the stimulus in the crea-
tion of relatively unorthodox forms of accommodation -
loft conversions and the like.

More than half of the decline in white population
was offset by an increase of 502,500 nonwhites. As a
result, New York City's nonwhite population has in-
creased its proportional share from 23.4 percent in
1970 to an estimated 31.5 percent in 1975. Every age
category took part in this expansion, with more than
two-thirds of it in the relatively youthful age

EXHIBIT 5-2
NEW YORK CITY POPULATION CHANGE
BY AGE AND COLOR: 1970 TO 1975

Age Category	July 1, 1970	July 1, 1975	Change: 1970 to 1975 Number	Percent
		TOTAL POPULATION		
TOTAL	7,893,551	7,490,690	-402,861	-5.1
<5	613,738	496,813	-116,925	-19.1
5-14	1,257,374	1,041,381	-215,993	-17.2
15-24	1,258,373	1,296,348	37,975	3.0
25-34	1,075,505	1,347,501	271,996	25.3
35-44	911,264	771,696	-139,568	-15.3
45-54	937,952	839,820	-98,132	-10.5
55-64	888,614	771,803	±116,811	-13.1
65 +	950,731	925,328	- 25,403	- 2.7
		WHITE POPULATION		
TOTAL	6,030,888	5,125,527	-905,361	-15.0
<5	419,024	263,827	-155,197	-37.0
5-14	852,775	568,434	-284,341	-33.3
15-24	938,318	843,047	- 95,271	-10.2
25-34	781,540	918,682	137,142	17.5
35-44	671,687	470,443	-201,244	-30.0
45-54	749,705	614,262	-135,443	-18.1
55-64	766,779	627,798	-138,981	-18.1
65+	851,060	819,034	- 32,026	- 3.8
		NONWHITE POPULATION		
TOTAL	1,862,663	2,365,163	502,500	27.0
<5	194,714	232,986	38,272	19.7
5-14	404,599	472,947	68,348	16.9
15-24	320,055	453,301	133,246	41.6
25-34	293,965	428,819	134,854	45.9
35-44	239,965	301,253	61,676	25.7
45-54	188,247	225,558	37,311	19.8
55-64	121,835	144,005	22,170	18.2
65+	99,671	106,294	6,623	6.6

Source: CUPR Projections

catagories under the age of 34 years. Indeed over half
of the 1975 nonwhite population was between 15 and 34
years of age. Thus, subject to migration, given the low
levels of natural attrition (high survival rates)
attached to this age span, and the relatively high fertility rates associated with it, a base is provided to
reinforce the nonwhite population's representation within the city. Indicative of this potential is the under-
5-years-of-age category, which as of 1975, was nearly
evenly distributed between whites and nonwhites.

1970 to 1975 Migration

The major determinant of this shift was the pattern
of migration. As shown in Exhibit 3, *the city suffered
a net migration loss of 576,656 individuals*, with the
total again obscuring the complex flows underlying it.
*There were over 935,000 more whites who left the city
than became residents of it, a loss only partially offset by the net inmigration of 358,782 nonwhites.* The
most striking decline, accounting for more than a third
of the former total, is in the under-15-years-of-age
category, serving as the complement of the departure of
relatively youthful household heads (35 to 44 years of
age).

Of equivalent significance is an abrupt increase in
the outmigration of the elderly, with more than 188,000
whites and a small but significant number of nonwhites
leaving the city. (Indeed this is the only nonwhite age
sector which evidenced outmigration.) It should be
noted in this context that to the degree that the migration of the elderly represents a highly selective phenomenon - i.e., those with the resources to make a geographic
shift of significant dimension - the resulting impact upon the city's fiscal base may be severe. In
general, the affluent elderly impose very little in the
way of municipal service costs on the city. Therefore,
their taxable expenditures, both direct and indirect,
represent a high proportion of net yield (revenues minus
costs) to the fiscal system. But not only is the immediate taxation of spending streams important in this context. The shifts of capital - of the accumulated wealth
of the elderly, particularly to the Sunbelt -- are difficult to document; nonetheless, their significance
should not be underestimated.[4]

Despite this flight, the city still served as a
mecca for youthful nonwhites, as indicated by the net
inmigration of 125,693 individuals in the 25-to 34-
years-of-age category, with an additional 93,634 in the

EXHIBIT 5-3
NEW YORK CITY MIGRATION TOTALS
BY AGE AND COLOR: 1970 TO 1975

Age Category	Total	White	Nonwhite
TOTAL	-576,656	-935,439	358,783
<5	- 61,382	- 68,933	7,551
5-14	-201,502	-271,178	69,676
15-24	73,164	- 20,470	93,634
25-34	105,622	- 20,071	125,693
35-44	-134,586	-179,751	45,165
45-54	- 77,937	- 94,398	16,461
55-64	- 91,209	- 97,667	6,458
65+	-188,826	-182,971	- 5,855

Note: Interval between July 1, 1970 and July 1, 1975.

Source: CUPR Projections.

15-to 24-year-old group. It should be noted that this
occurred during a period in which the city's employment opportunities were sharply curtailed.

The Components of Change: 1970 to 1975

What are the relative weights of migration and net
natural increase in the overall process of population
change? The data in Exhibit 4 appear sufficient to
probe this question. For the city as a whole, only in
the 25-to 34-years-of-age sector does the magnitude of
net natural increase exceed that of migration. Indeed,
*the total net natural increase of 173,795 on a popula-
tion base of 7.5 million people is relatively incon-
sequential.* Yet, since the directional pattern for all
categories was negative, with the exceptions of the 25-
to 34-year-old group earlier cited and the elderly, the
net natural increase variable acted to amplify the effects of migration.

The pattern of insufficient internal replacement
is, as would be expected, most marked for the white
sector. *The total white net natural increase was
30,000 with only the baby boom cohort, and the elderly,
demonstrating positive increments.* Yet these gains
were sufficient to offset the decreases evident for the
remaining age sectors. It is particularly important
in this context to note the decline as a function of
net natural increase in the under-5-years-of-age
category - of the total shrinkage in this preschool
category (-155,197), over 86,000 can be attributed to
net natural decrease.

*The contrast across the nonwhite age groups is
evident where the total net natural increase (143,717
individuals) wielded considerably more force.* Despite
a decline in the overall birth rates of the nonwhite
populace, there was a net natural increase of over
30,000 children under the age of 5 years, a consequence of the continued expansion in size of the childbearing sectors. Moreover, for every age group, except that between 5 and 14 years, population gains were
registered through the process of net natural increase,
reinforcing those secured through migration. The relatively youthful segment between 15 and 24 years of
age - destined to emerge as heads of households and
the parents of children - experienced the largest gain
(39,612 individuals). When that number is added to the
net inmigration of 93,634, a truly formidable age cohort materializes, one whose impact will be felt in the
future.

EXHIBIT 5-4
NEW YORK CITY, COMPONENTS OF POPULATION CHANGE, BY AGE AND COLOR: 1970 TO 1975

Age Category	Total Population Change	Migration	Net Natural Increase
TOTAL POPULATION			
TOTAL	-402,861	-576,656	173,795
<5	-116,925	- 61,382	- 55,543
5-14	-215,993	-201,502	- 14,491
15-24	37,975	73,164	- 35,189
25-34	271,996	105,622	166,374
35-44	-139,568	-134,586	- 4,982
45-54	- 98,132	- 77,937	- 20,195
55-64	-116,811	- 91,209	- 25,602
65+	- 25,403	-188,826	163,432
WHITE POPULATION			
TOTAL	-905,361	-935,439	30,078
<5	-155,197	- 68,933	- 86,264
5-14	-284,341	-271,178	- 13,163
15-24	- 95,271	- 20,470	- 74,801
25-34	137,142	- 20,071	157,213
35-44	-201,244	-179,751	- 21,493
45-54	-135,443	- 94,398	- 41,045
55-64	-138,981	- 97,667	- 41,314
65+	- 32,026	-182,971	150,945
NONWHITE POPULATION			
TOTAL	502,500	358,783	143,717
<5	38,272	7,551	30,721
5-14	68,348	69,676	- 1,328
15-24	133,246	93,634	39,612
25-34	134,854	125,693	9,161
35-44	61,676	45,165	16,511
45-54	37,311	16,461	20,850
55-64	22,170	6,458	15,712
65+	6,623	- 5,855	12,478

Note: Interval between July 1, 1970 and July 1, 1975.

Source: CUPR Projections.

The Broader Context

In order to place the age structure pattern of New York City within the national context, Exhibit 5 presents the profiles and percentage changes for 1970 to 1975 for both geographical areas. A major divergence lies in the comparative paucity of children under the age of 15 years in the city, where their proportional share of the total population is barely one in five; in the nation, their proportional share is one in four. This differential is largely counterbalanced by New York City's relatively high concentration of people in the 25-to 34-years-of-age category, which encompasses 18 percent of the city's population, as compared to 14.5 percent for the nation.

Clearly, this bulge will prove significant for the city's future. The provision of housing accommodations unique and distinctive enough to appeal to this age sector is an effort that, rather than being a fight against the tide, i.e., a struggle to bring back families with children, has a strong predisposition working for it.

The dynamics of change in New York and the nation are indicated at the bottom of Exhibit 5. Again, the sheer force of the baby boom dominates the pattern of change. In both areas, the largest percentage gains were the province of the 25-to 34-years-of-age sectors. While the directional patterns of change were similar for those age brackets below 45 years, a distinctive feature of New York City's demography was the contraction in size of those segments of the population 45 years of age and older.

Summary

The changes in New York City's population over the 1970 to 1975 period - as those of its economic base - appear unprecedented in modern historical annals. However, it is not the shape and pattern of change that are surprising, but their severity. Their outline could have been perceived from the evidence of the previous decade; their scale of import could not. Nonetheless, the major dimensions of the trends in force are as follows:

EXHIBIT 5-5
AGE STRUCTURE PATTERNS
NEW YORK CITY AND THE UNITED STATES: JULY 1, 1975
(Numbers in thousands)

	Total	<5	5-14	15-24	25-34	35-44	45-54	55-64	65+
				AGE CATEGORY					
United States	213,540	15,882	37,734	40,244	30,918	22,815	23,768	19,774	22,405
New York City	7,491	497	1,041	1,296	1,348	772	840	772	925
				PERCENT DISTRIBUTION					
United States	100.0	7.4	17.4	18.8	14.5	10.7	11.1	9.3	10.5
New York City	100.0	6.6	13.9	17.3	18.0	10.3	11.2	10.3	12.2
				PERCENT CHANGE: 1970 TO 1975					
United States	5.1	- 7.4	- 7.4	13.6	24.1	- 1.2	2.4	6.4	11.7
New York City	- 5.1	-19.3	-17.1	3.5	25.3	-15.7	- 10.8	-13.3	- 2.4

Source: CUPR Projections; U.S. Bureau of the Census, Current Population Reports, Series P-25, No. 706, "Estimates of the Population of the United States and Components of Change: 1940 to 1976," U.S. Government Printing Office, Washington, D.C., 1977.

1. *In the 1970 to 1975 period, the city's population is projected to have fallen from 7,893,551 to 7,490,690, a loss of 402,861 people or 5.1 percent.*

2. *The only age-specific subpopulations that demonstrate growth are the correlates of the baby boom cohorts for this time period, the 15-to 34-years-of-age sectors. All other age groups of the total population show declines, with the major losses attached to the age sectors in periods of low fertility - the baby bust generation (under 14 years of age) and the Depression era progeny (35 to 44 years of age).*

3. *When the city's population is segmented by white/nonwhite partitions, the complexity underlying the city's transition is emphasized. The overall decline is the end result of whites rapidly vacating the city (-905,361 individuals) and an insufficient number of nonwhite replacements (502,500). Therefore, partial vacuums are opening up, physically documented by expanding landscapes of abandoned buildings.*

4. *The changing age structure of the white population generally mirrors the overall city pattern. Gains were secured only by the 25-to 34-years-of-age sector. In marked contrast, every nonwhite age group manifested positive growth increments.*

5. *Other elements of the dynamic underlying the overall city experience are revealed by the components of population change - migration and net natural increase.*

   a) The city suffers a net migration loss of 576,656 individuals, which cuts across all age sectors except those between 15 and 34 years of age. However, the white/ nonwhite migration flows diverge. The former shows a net outmigration of 935,439 people while the latter experiences a net inmigration of 358,783 individuals. The white outflow is again spearheaded by what we infer to be family-raising households and the nonwhite inflow is composed mainly of young individuals under 35 years of age.

*b) The total net natural increase
(173,795) falls far short of countering
the total migration loss. For the city
as a whole, and the white sector, the
only age groups showing positive natural
increase components are the 25-to 34-
(the maturing baby boom residuals) and
the over-64-years-of-age categories.
Positive gains characterize the nonwhite
age structure, excepting only the 5 to 14
years of age sector (which encompasses the
baby bust cohort).*

6. *These changes bear the imprint not only of
historical momentum, but also of forces
evidenced on a national scale. The New York
City experience of the 1970 to 1975 period
- in terms of age structure shifts - generally
corresponds to the national pattern; yet the
age-specific changes are much more pronounced
in the city.*

THE 1975 TO 1980 PERIOD

As we move into future time intervals, the validity of the projection results rests not only on the
limitations of the methodological underpinnings, but
also on the degree to which extraneous variables do not
nullify the underlying assumptions. An abrupt weaken-
ing of the international competitiveness of the nation's
economy, an unforeseen depression, a substantial shift
in energy costs, and major alterations in government
expenditure policies are just a few of the external elements that could substantially alter the data that are
presented here. Nevertheless, the basic trendlines,
both in terms of total population and white/nonwhite
growth patterns, are very powerful and have gained considerable momentum. A substantial deflection of their
trajectory may be occasioned only under the most ex-
traordinary of social and economic circumstances. The
projections, therefore, should be viewed as subject to
external modification, but having a high probability of
matching future reality. With these stipulations in
mind, attention will be fully directed to the 1975 to
1980 period.

*First, and primarily, it is one in which the
population decline of the city, while continuing, does
so at a much abated level. Indeed, the loss that is
projected falls below 100,000 individuals (See Exhibit
6).* Again, the patterns of change are age related,

EXHIBIT 5-6
NEW YORK CITY POPULATION CHANGE,
BY AGE AND COLOR: 1975 TO 1980

Age Category	July 1, 1975	July 1, 1980	Change: 1975-1980 Number	Percent
TOTAL POPULATION				
TOTAL	7,490,690	7,391,510	-99,180	- 1.3
< 5	496,813	519,854	23,041	4.6
5-14	1,041,381	832,302	-209,079	20.1
15-24	1,296,348	1,273,863	-22,485	- 1.7
25-34	1,347,501	1,568,478	220,977	16.4
35-44	771,696	875,558	103,862	13.5
45-54	839,820	701,291	-138,529	-16.5
55-64	771,803	698,555	-73,248	- 9.5
65+	925,328	921,609	- 3,719	- 0.4
WHITE POPULATION				
TOTAL	5,125,527	4,426,680	-698,847	-13.6
< 5	263,827	256,172	- 7,655	- 2.9
5-14	568,434	299,268	-269,166	-47.4
15-24	843,047	681,162	-161,885	-19.2
25-34	918,682	980,681	61,999	6.7
35-44	470,443	465,444	- 4,999	- 1.1
45-54	614,262	435,654	-178,608	-29.1
55-64	627,798	520,699	-107,099	-17.1
65+	819,034	787,600	-31,434	- 3.8
NONWHITE POPULATION				
TOTAL	2,365,163	2,964,830	599,667	25.4
< 5	232,986	263,682	30,696	13.2
5-14	472,947	533,034	60,087	12.7
15-24	453,301	492,701	139,400	30.8
25-34	428,819	589,797	158,978	37.1
35-44	301,253	410.114	108,861	36.1
45-54	225,558	265,637	40,079	17.8
55-64	144,005	177,856	33,851	23.5
65+	106,294	134,009	27,715	26.1

Source: CUPR Projections.

and are largely a function of a decrease of more than
200,000 individuals in the 5-to 14-years-of-age category and an equivalent decline attached to the 45-to 64-
years-of-age bracket. These losses more than offset
the increase secured by the 25-to 44-years-of-age category, into which the surging baby boom cohorts have
fully matured. The other age sectors typically show
small losses with the exception of a marginal increase
in the under-5-years-of-age subpopulation.

Again, the changes reflected by the overall population mask a significant transformation of the city's
white/nonwhite composition. Over the five-year period,
the former declines by more than one in eight; the latter
increases at double that ratio - one in four. *Consequently, nonwhites, who comprised 31.6 percent of the
population in 1975 should represent 40.1 percent of New
York City's residents by 1980.*

The white population decline is most evident again
in the 5-to 14-years-of-age category, which exhibited
a loss of 47.4 percent. This is the continuation of the
decline characterizing the 0 to 14 years of age sectors
during the 1970 to 1975 time period. Similarly, despite
the overall increase in the under-5-years-of-age category between 1975 and 1980, the white portion continues
to decline both in share (now falling into an absolute
minority) and in number, although the rate of white decline (-2.9 percent) diminishes appreciably from that
registered during the preceding five years (-37.0 percent). While the only age category among whites that
continues to expand is the 25- to 34-years-of-age group,
it should be noted that the leading edge of the baby
boom cohort has entered the 35-to 44-years-of-age category, mitigating the shrinkage of the latter. Nonetheless, despite a generally aging population, the number of whites 65 years old and over declined in number,
with a net loss in excess of 30,000 people.

Of particular significance is the reduction in
white potential newcomers to the labor force, synon-
omous with the 15-to 24-years-of-age category, which
shows a decline of nearly 162,000 individuals. Both
the opportunity and the challenge of accommodating
this reality - of substituting nonwhite employees for
their white equivalents - are most evident. If the
city's newcomers to the labor force are limited to its
residents, fewer of these will be white and more of
them will be nonwhite. A major question is whether
the transition can be made in an effective manner.

Certainly, the 139,400 person increase projected for nonwhites between the ages of 15 to 24 years will tax much of our society's adjustment capacity. Indeed, in absolute number, this is the largest growth sector other than that immediately senior to it, the 25- to 34-years-of-age group. Together these two account for 50 percent of the total increase in nonwhite population.

The period of highest fertility spans between 15 and 29 years of age. Approximating this interval with the 15-to 24-years-of-age sector, the elements of continuity in demographic extrapolation become most evident. The white subpopulation of this age in 1980 (681,162) barely exceeds the magnitude of their nonwhite counterparts (592,701). Significantly, over the 1975 to 1980 period, the former declined by 161,885 individuals while the latter increased by 60,087. With nonwhites evidencing a higher rate of fertility, the birth producing capacity of the two groups reaches parity by 1980, a reality already documented in the under-5-years-of-age sectors. The full import of this transformation will be revealed in the succeeding time interval.

1975 to 1980 Migration

The changes evidenced over this period once again reveal the import of the migration variable, although the outmigration eases, totaling 367,000 people (See Exhibit 7), *approximately 200,000 less than that of the 1970 to 1975 period.* This deficit is accounted for by both ends of the age spectrum, with the bulk of the losses accruing to the under-14-years- and 65-years-and-over age sectors; net outmigration is also characteristic of the population between 35 and 64 years of age. Only in the 15-to 34-years-of-age sectors is there a positive migration balance. However, it is nowhere near sufficient in size to counter the substantial losses attached to the other age sectors.

Total migration, however, is but the residual of the movements of the white and nonwhite subpopulations. The gross pattern of net outmigration, however, is attributable to the former - *the projected net outmigration of whites exceeds 783,000,* with every age sector partaking in the phenomenon. In contrast, positive migration balances are secured by every nonwhite age category, except that 65 years of age and over. *In total nonwhites reflect a net inmigration of over 416,000 individuals.*

EXHIBIT 5-7
NEW YORK CITY MIGRATION TOTALS
BY AGE AND COLOR: 1975 TO 1980

Age Category	Total	White	Nonwhite
TOTAL	-366,932	-783,409	416,427
5	- 49,004	- 57,777	8,773
5-14	-146,339	-227,291	80,952
15-24	102,539	- 6,248	108,787
25-34	140,874	- 5,171	146,045
35-44	- 98,185	-150,660	52,475
45-54	- 59,996	- 79,121	19,125
55-64	- 74,357	- 81,860	7,503
65+	-182,514	-175,281	- 7,233

Note: Interval between July 1, 1975 and July 1, 1980.

Source: CUPR Projections.

As discussed more fully in the methodology, the
pace of nonwhite inmigration may be substantially altered as a function of increased job opportunities for
these groups in the South, which will, in turn, be substantially a function of national employment policy.
However, if the dynamics presently at work are not
deflected, the results as presented here are likely to
be realized.

The Components of Change: 1975 to 1980

The interaction between the migration and net
natural increase parameters evolves quite markedly in
the 1975 to 1980 period (See Exhibit 8). While the
former is still considerably more potent than the latter,
the gap between the two narrows appreciably. Migration
is projected to shrink from its 1970 to 1975 levels, while
the net natural increase component increases in absolute
size. The growth of the latter is the consequence of
many factors, several of which are clear echoes of the
postwar baby boom. They emerge first in the growth of
the 25-to 44-years-of-age categories, and second as a
derivative wave of births (the under-5-years-of-age
sector), a result of the expansion in the number of
women of childbearing age. The increase in births - and
hence net natural increase - is also a consequence of
the changing color composition of the city - relatively
youthful nonwhites of childbearing age replacing whites
who are external to that category.

The toll that these transformation exact - in terms
of rapid change buffeting the city - is clearly evident.
The white net natural increase of 84,562 individuals is
the province of three distinct age groups, two of which
have been noted above - the baby boom cohorts (falling
within the 25-to 44-years-of-age sectors) and their offspring (under 5 years of age). Additionally, the white
elderly (65 years and over) secured gains through net
natural increase. But the only case in which net
natural increase is in excess of migration is in the 25-
to 34-years-of-age category. Even the abrupt natural
increase in the elderly is more than offset by migration.

The pattern of nonwhite net natural increase
(183,240) is pervasive across the age spectrum, with
the only deviation in the 5-to 14-years-of-age sector,
which gauges the contracting birth rates of the 1965 to
1975 period (with the growth in the number of nonwhite
females in the childbearing years for the latter period
not sufficient to maintain the high level of births.)

EXHIBIT 5-8
NEW YORK CITY, COMPONENTS OF POPULATION
CHANGE, BY AGE AND COLOR: 1975 TO 1980

Age Category	Total Population Change	Migration	Net Natural Increase
	TOTAL POPULATION		
TOTAL	- 99,180	-366,982	267,802
< 5	23,041	- 49,004	72,045
5-14	-209,079	-146,339	- 62,740
15-24	- 22,485	102,539	-125,024
25-34	220,977	140,874	80,103
35-44	103,862	- 98,185	202,047
45-54	-138,529	- 59,996	- 78,533
55-64	- 73,248	- 74,357	1,109
65+	- 3,719	-182,514	178,795
	WHITE POPULATION		
TOTAL	-698,847	-783,409	84,562
<5	- 7,655	- 57,777	50,122
5-14	-269,166	-227,291	- 41,875
15-24	-161,885	- 6,248	-155,637
25-34	61,999	- 5,171	67,170
35-44	- 4,999	-150,660	145,661
45-54	-178,608	- 79,121	- 99,487
55-64	-107,099	- 81,860	- 25,239
65+	- 31,434	-175,281	143,847
	NONWHITE POPULATION		
TOTAL	599,667	416,427	183,240
< 5	30,696	8,773	21,923
5-14	60,087	80,952	- 20,865
15-24	139,400	108,787	30,865
25-34	158,978	146,045	12,933
35-44	108,861	52,475	56,386
45-54	40,079	19,125	20,954
55-64	33,851	7,503	26,348
65+	27,715	- 7,233	34,948

Note: Interval between July 1, 1975 and July 1, 1980.

Source: CUPR Projections.

Hence the decline in the number of 5 to 14 year olds,
for example, is a function of the past decline in
fertility rates among nonwhites; the increment in the
under-5-years-of-age category is a function of the
radical growth in the number of women in the childbearing ages over the 1975 to 1980 period. *Despite
this deviation, the conjunction of migration and net
natural increase-total population change - generates
pressures within the city of adjusting to a much higher
proportion of nonwhites among newcomers to the labor
force. The potential is evident; the issue of ful-
filling that potential, clearly challenging.*

The Broader Context

Once again, it is useful to take a broader evaluative stance by summarizing the changes anticipated
within the city in the context of projections for the
United States as a whole (See Exhibit 9). The revitalization of New York City's demography with a population of high fertility is shown by the proportion of
population under the age of 5 years - 7 percent in New
York City versus 6.6 percent in the nation, a sharp
repositioning of past patterns. This is partly a result
of the complementary increment in the 25-to 44-years-
of-age categories, which in New York will represent
nearly a third of the population (33.1 percent) and in
the United States as a whole, 28.1 percent.

In the context of total population change, the
city clearly will lag the nation. While projections
for the latter show growth on the order of 3.4 percent,
the city's rate of decline is projected at 1.3 percent.
Throughout the age continuum of both areas, the broader
phenomena of baby boom and baby bust are manifested
clearly in the rates of change of their respective cohorts. Despite these similarities, major deviations
are present, principally in the age sectors above 45
years. Here the national-local gaps are substantial,
and may reveal the vacation of the city by that portion
of its citizenry of greatest economic capacity.

Summary

A dampening and gradual abatement in the severity
of the early 1970s trendlines is the dominant theme of
the 1975 to 1980 period. Yet the city is still enmeshed in the throes of profound change in its demographic matrix.

EXHIBIT 5-9
AGE STRUCTURE PATTERNS
NEW YORK CITY AND THE UNITED STATES: JULY 1, 1980
(Numbers in thousands)

	Total	< 5	5-14	15-24	25-34	35-44	45-54	55-64	65+
				AGE CATEGORY					
United States	220,732	14,593	33,896	41,527	36,172	25,721	22,698	21,198	24,927
New York City	7,392	520	832	1,274	1,568	876	701	699	922
				PERCENT DISTRIBUTION					
United States	100.0	6.6	15.4	18.8	16.4	11.7	10.3	9.6	11.3
New York City	100.0	7.0	11.3	17.2	21.2	11.9	9.5	9.5	12.5
				PERCENT CHANGE: 1975 TO 1980					
United States	3.4	- 8.1	-10.2	3.2	17.0	12.7	- 4.5	7.2	11.3
New York City	- 1.3	4.6	-20.1	-1.7	16.3	13.5	-16.5	-9.5	- 9.3

Sources: CUPR Projections; U.S. Bureau of the Census, Current Population Reports, Series P-25, No. 704, "Projections of the Population of the United States: 1977 to 2050," U.S. Government Printing Office, Washington, D.C. 1977.

1. The population level of the city falls from
    7,480,690 in 1975 to 7,391,510 in 1980, a
    decline of 99,180 people or 1.3 percent. The
    age sectors that maintain growth tend to be
    somewhat older than their counterparts of the
    preceding period (25 to 44 years of age ver-
    sus 15 to 34 years of age) underscoring the
    aging of the baby boom generation. And, as
    a derivative function of the latter, an
    increase in the under-5-years-of-age popula-
    tion occurs. All other age sectors are
    characterized by declines.

2. One of the crosscurrents underlying the over-
    all city experience is defined by the persis-
    tent transitions of its white/nonwhite sub-
    populations.

        a) The white sector loses 698,847 indi-
        viduals (-13.6 percent) as its total falls
        to the 4.4 million person level. The
        maturing baby boom cohorts provide the
        only relief from pervasive declines across
        its entire age profile.

        b) The nonwhite population increase
        (599,667 people) fails to offset com-
        pletely the white decline. Nonetheless,
        by 1980, nonwhites comprise 40.1 percent
        of the city's population, as compared to
        31.6 percent in 1975. The gains are
        registered across the entire nonwhite
        age spectrum.

3. The white/nonwhite transition during this
    period is underscored by the patterns of mi-
    gration. The overall city migration exper-
    ience (-266,982 people) is the result of a
    net outflow of 783,409 whites and a net in-
    migration of 416,427 nonwhites. These con-
    flicting patterns of movement are representa-
    tive of the experience of virtually every age
    group of the respective subpopulations.

4. While the overall migration total of the 1975
    to 1980 period (-366,982) is considerably
    smaller than that projected for the preceding
    five years (-576,656), the net natural in-
    crease secured during the 1975 to 1980 period
    (267,802) is greater than that experienced
    from 1970 to 1975 (173,795). Yet, the gap
    between the two components remains, defined
    by continued absolute population losses for
    the city.

a) The white natural increase is attributed to the surviving populations bolstering the ranks of the elderly (65 years of age and over), the inertia of the baby boom (25 to 44 years of age), and the wave of derivative births (under 5 years of age) emanating from the latter. This pattern is analogous to that displayed by the city's population in total.

b) The total white net natural increase (84,562) stands in marked contrast to that of nonwhites (183,240). For the most part, the natural increase gains of the nonwhite population are characteristic of each of its age groups, reinforcing the growth dynamic established by migration.

5. *General correspondence with the projected national age structure changes is again evident. The major differences are the consequence of both the evolution of past variations - the city's traditional losses among its more mature citizenry are now unique only above 55 years of age - and the pyramiding effect of more recent developments - the positive growth in the city's under-5-years-of-age population due to the increasing critical mass of the nonwhite population.*

THE 1980 TO 1985 PERIOD

The path of projection becomes much more hazardous as the time span lengthens further into the future. Tangential deviations which are slight in the short term tend to pyramid into much larger consequences in the long term. Recognizing this admonition, if it is nonetheless assumed that the trends portrayed through 1980 were to continue through 1985, the demographic results would be similar to those shown in Exhibit 10. *The city as a whole encounters a slight increase in population decline, compared to the previous five years, with a loss of 160,312 individuals, 2.2 percent of the 1980 base.* As will be noted in more detail subsequently, the accelerating erosion of the city's population base takes place despite a projected dampening in the rate of decline of the city's economic base. This dilemma results from continued labor force expansion, which,

EXHIBIT 5-10
NEW YORK CITY POPULATION CHANGE,
BY AGE AND COLOR: 1980 TO 1985

Age Category	July 1, 1980	July 1, 1985	Change: 1980-1985 Number	Percent
TOTAL POPULATION				
TOTAL	7,391,510	7,231,198	-160,312	- 2.2
< 5	519,854	527,984	8,130	1.6
5-14	832,302	742,535	- 89,767	-10.8
15-24	1,273,863	1,082,822	-192,041	-15.0
25-34	1,568,478	1,620,530	52,052	3.3
35-44	875,558	1,163,284	287,726	32.9
45-54	701,291	585,808	-115,483	-16.5
55-64	698,555	619,076	- 79,479	-11.4
65+	921,609	889,159	- 32,450	- 3.5
WHITE POPULATION				
TOTAL	4,426,680	3,675,773	-750,907	-17.0
< 5	256,172	225,209	- 30,963	-12.1
5-14	299,268	143,060	-156,208	-52.2
15-24	681,162	417,631	-263,531	-38.7
25-34	980,681	892;646	- 88,035	- 9.0
35-44	465,444	613,620	148,176	31.8
45-54	435,654	257,916	-177,738	-24.2
55-64	520,699	405,782	-114,917	-22.1
65+	787,600	719,909	- 67,691	- 8.6
NONWHITE POPULATION				
TOTAL	2,964,830	3,555,425	590,595	19.9
< 5	263,682	302,775	39,093	14.8
5-14	533,034	599,475	66,441	12.5
15-24	592,701	665,191	72,490	12.2
25-34	587,797	727,884	140,087	23.8
35-44	410,114	549,664	139,550	34.0
45-54	265,637	327,892	62,255	23.4
55-64	177,856	213,294	35,438	19.9
65+	134,009	169,250	35,241	26.3

Source: CUPR Projections.

despite the induced outmigration of the preceeding
projection interval, widens the gap between the supply
and demand subsectors, generating increased outmigration for the 1980 to 1985 period. Even if the city's
job base were to remain stable over the first five
years of the 1980s, outmigration would still be preci-
pitated, since - according to the premises of the underlying model structure - a labor force supply exceeding
the capacity of the economic base initiates the migration flow.

Despite this unique local situation, the parameters of change are still dominated by the continued
elaboration of historical national phenomena. As detailed in Exhibit 10, the changes projected for the 1980
to 1985 period reflect the sustained maturation of the
baby boom progeny - whose cohorts will be between 28
and 39 years of age by 1985.[5] Hence the 25-to 44-years-
of-age categories still show growth for this period.
Offsetting these gains are the losses attached to the
5-to 24-years-of-age categories, which encompass the
aging baby bust, and the 45-years-of-age and over sectors, the loss of which is an extension of New York
City's unique historical trendline - the vacation of
the city by the more mature age segments among its
populace.

The relatively small decline in total city population occurs despite a striking decrease once again
in the number and proportion of whites. *Their projected losses (750,907 people) leave them only a very
small majority (50.8 percent) in the context of the
city's total population.* Decline is pervasive across
all age sectors, with the exception of the growth projected in the 35-to 44-years-of-age category, the leading edge of the baby boom. The shrinkage is most
severe in the 5-to 24-years-of-age category, into which
the baby bust fully penetrates by 1985.

*The nonwhite population in 1985 will account for
49.2 percent of the city's total population and, in a
number of age categories will assume a distinct majority status.* Positive growth increments are characteristic of every nonwhite age category with a slight
aging of the growth curve evident, i.e., the largest
gains are secured by the over-25-years-of-age categories.

If the projected trendlines evolve into concrete
reality - if they represent the future - the population
of New York City under 25 years of age in 1985 will be
predominantly nonwhite. Only in selected instances - at
the elderly extremes of the age continuum - will the
white population represent a strong majority. The
changing internal composition of the city will become an
ever more visible phenomenon.

1980-1985 Migration

It should by now be readily apparent that the
above changes represent the intersection of the forces
of historical inertia with the more variable migrational
components. Again, the latter continues to exert a powerful influence on the evolution of the city's demography.
As shown in Exhibit 11, *the projections indicate a net
outmigration of whites in excess of 830,700, distributed
across every age category. Nonwhite net inmigration
(379,908 individuals) offsets less than half of the white
outflow.* Indeed, only in the age span between 15 and 34
years is the nonwhite inmigration sufficient to yield
a net positive increment for the city as a whole. Every
remaining age sector of the *total population* is characterized by net outmigration, which, when aggregated,
exceeds 450,800 people.

The Components of Change: 1980 to 1985

*The increased net migration of this period
(-450,812) stands in contrast to that projected for
the 1975 to 1980 period (-366,982). Its translation
into total population change is mitigated partially by
the gains secured through net natural increase (290,500
in the 1980 to 1985 period versus 267,802 over the preceding five years).* (See Exhibit 12.) Again this is
the consequence of the growth in the number of females
of childbearing age, together with higher projected
birth rates attendant to the nonwhite sector (in comparison to their white counterparts). *Indeed, only 27.5
percent of the total net natural increase is white
(79,813 out of 290,500).*

For both the population in total, and the white
subsector the major gains achieved in net natural increase are the province of the maturing baby boom
bulge (captured by the 35-to 44-years-of-age category),
the births emanating from the latter over the preceding decade (reflected in the 14-years-of-age and-un-
der groups), and the growth of the elderly (65 years

EXHIBIT 5-11
NEW YORK CITY MIGRATION TOTALS
BY AGE AND COLOR: 1980 TO 1985

Age Category	Total	White	Nonwhite
TOTAL	-450,812	-830,720	379,908
< 5	- 54,461	- 62,515	8,054
5-14	-171,620	-245,933	74,313
15-24	86,658	- 13,206	99,864
25-34	121,611	-,12,455	134,066
35-44	-114,844	-163,016	48,172
45-54	- 68,054	- 85,611	17,557
55-64	- 81,687	- 88,575	6,888
65+	-168,415	-159,409	- 9,006

Note: Interval between July 1, 1980 and July 1, 1985.

Source: CUPR Projections.

EXHIBIT 5-12
NEW YORK CITY, COMPONENTS OF POPULATION CHANGE BY AGE AND COLOR: 1980 TO 1985

Age Category	Total Population Change	Migration	Net Natural Increase
TOTAL POPULATION			
TOTAL	-160,312	-450,812	290,500
< 5	8,130	- 54,461	62,591
5-14	- 89,767	-171,620	81,853
15-24	-191,041	86,658	-277,699
25-34	52,052	121,611	- 69,559
35-44	287,726	-114,844	402,570
45-54	-115,483	- 68,054	- 47,429
55-64	- 79,479	- 81,687	2,208
65+	- 32,450	-168,415	135,965
WHITE POPULATION			
TOTAL	-750,907	-830,720	79,813
< 5	- 30,963	- 62,515	31,552
5-14	-156,208	-245,933	89,725
15-24	-263,531	- 13,206	-250,325
25-34	- 88,035	- 12,455	- 75,580
35-44	148,176	-163,016	311,192
45-54	-177,738	- 85,611	- 92,127
55-64	-114,917	- 88,575	- 26,342
65+	- 67,691	-159,409	91,718
NONWHITE POPULATION			
TOTAL	590,595	379,908	210,687
< 5	39,093	8,054	31,039
5-14	66,441	74,313	- 7,872
15-24	72,490	99,864	- 27,374
25-34	140,087	134,066	6,021
35-44	139,550	48,172	91,378
45-54	62,255	17,557	44,698
55-64	35,438	6,888	28,698
65+	35,241	- 9,006	44,247

Note: Interval between July 1, 1980 and July 1, 1985.
Source: CUPR Projections.

of age and over). The major net natural decreases
center about the leading edge of the baby bust generation (15 to 24 years of age) and the Depression era
products (45 to 54 years of age). *It is important to
note in this context that the total white net natural
increase (79,813) compensates for only 9.6 percent of
the total white net outmigration (-830,720).*

   In contrast, *the nonwhite net natural increase
(210,687) serves to bolster the effect of the migrational component (379,908), generating a total nonwhite
growth increment of 590,595 people.* Only the residual
effects of the baby bust (encompassed principally in
the 15-to 24-years-of-age sector) mars the overall
pattern of sustained nonwhite net natural increase.

The Broader Context

   A comparison of the projected age structures of
New York City and the nation are presented in Exhibit
13. Despite the maturation of the nonwhite population
of the city - which may be rapidly assuming the characteristics of the white population at an earlier stage
of the city's history - New York is proportionally
underrepresented in the older age groups (45 years of
age and over) when compared to the national baseline.
Nonetheless, the overall age structure patterns exhibit
considerable correspondence. However, the city does
stand unique in terms of the heavy concentration of
its population between 25 and 44 years of age.

   The changes inherent to this time frame (1980
to 1985) still are dominated by the historical cycles
of baby boom and baby bust. Yet these cycles are working themselves out in a national setting characterized
by growth (a 3.7 percent increase in total population)
and in a local setting of long-term decline (a -2.2
percent change in total New York City population.)

Summary

   The abated levels of population decline of the
1975 to 1980 period served as a brief interlude pre-
saging the greater losses projected between 1980 and
1985. However, the latter still do not approach in
scale the traumatic events of the 1970 to 1975 era.
Additionally, the experience of the 1980 to 1985 period
adds emphasis to a phenomenon often obscured: while
the rate of economic decline is the smallest of any

EXHIBIT 5-13
AGE STRUCTURE PATTERNS
NEW YORK CITY AND THE UNITED STATES: JULY 1, 1985
(Numbers in thousands)

	Total	< 5	5-14	15-24	25-34	35-44	45-54	55-64	65+
				AGE CATEGORY					
United States	228,879	16,235	31,394	38,517	39,859	31,376	22,457	21,737	27,305
New York City	7,231	528	743	1,083	1,620	1,163	586	619	889
				PERCENT DISTRIBUTION					
United States	100.0	7.1	13.7	16.8	17.4	13.7	9.8	9.5	11.9
New York City	100.0	7.3	10.3	15.0	22.4	16.1	8.1	8.5	12.3
				PERCENT CHANGE: 1980 TO 1985					
United States	3.7	11.3	- 7.4	- 7.2	10.2	22.0	- 1.1	2.5	9.5
New York City	- 2.2	1.5	-10.7	-15.0	3.3	32.8	-16.4	-11.4	-3.6

Source: CUPR Projections; U.S. Bureau of the Census, Current Population Reports, Series P-25, No. 704, "Projections of the Population of the United States: 1977 to 2050," U.S. Government Printing Office, Washington, D.C. 1977.

projection period, the persistence with which the labor
force expands maintains the impetus toward outmigration,
which in turn drains the city of valuable population
resources.

1. *Over the 1980 to 1985 period, the city's
    projected population losses (160,312 people)
    reduce the overall total to the 7.2 million
    person level. The nonwhite population in-
    crease (590,595), in which each of its age
    groups partakes, is considerably outweighed
    by the size of the white losses (-750,907).
    Within the latter subpopulation, the only
    age sector to experience growth is the 35 to
    44 years of age sector, into which the lead-
    ing edge of the baby boom has moved.*

2. *The nonwhite population gains virtual parity
    in terms of proportional representation (49.2
    percent). In those age sectors under 24 years
    of age, the nonwhite dominance is pronounced.
    In the more mature age spans, whites are still
    in the majority.*

3. *The projected increase in outmigration (-450,812
    is the result of the phenomenon discussed above.
    However, the total masks the significance of
    the unrelenting pace of white outmigration
    (-830,720) which exceeds the replacement capa-
    city of the nonwhite inflow (379,908).*

4. *The translation of the migration loss into
    absolute population decline is partially
    buffered by the growing size of the net
    natural increase component (290,500). In -
    creasingly, however, the latter is weighted
    toward the nonwhite sector - 210,687 nonwhites
    as against 79,813 whites.*

5. *Comparisons between the projected age struc-
    ture of the nation and that of the city show
    New York having a much greater proportion of
    its population falling between the ages of 25
    to 44 years. The 1980 to 1985 changes pro-
    jected for each area show similar patterns,
    but somewhat divergent magnitudes.*

EXHIBIT 5-14
NEW YORK CITY POPULATION BY AGE:
1970 TO 1985[1]

Age Category	1970	1975	1980	1985
TOTAL	7,893,551	7,490,690	7,391,510	7,231,198
5	613,738	496,813	519,854	527,984
5-14	1,257,374	1,041,381	832,802	742,535
15-24	1,258,373	1,296,348	1,273,863	1,084,822
25-34	1,075,505	1,347,501	1,568,478	1,620,530
35-44	911,264	771,696	875,558	1,163,284
45-54	937,952	839,820	701,291	585,808
55-64	888,614	771,803	698,555	619,076
65+	950,731	925,328	921,609	889,159

Note: 1.   As of July 1, of the reported years.

Source: CUPR Projections.

Further Discussion

The data in Exhibit 14 summarize the changes that occur in the city's age structure between 1970 and 1985. When displayed in absolute numbers for each of the terminal years, the tendency toward an increasing concentration of the population in the central age sectors is emphasized. Moreover, the evolution to the final pattern is clear - the gradual aging of the largest initial sectors into the 25-to 44-years-of-age category by 1985, the general depletion of the younger age groups, and the continued declines experienced by the more mature population elements of the city.

It is important to note that at each of these stages the population between the ages of 5 to 14 years of age exceeds that between the ages of 55 to 64 years. In each successive period the former provides the new entrants into the labor force while the latter begin to exit (ignoring for the moment the effects of changing participation rates.)[6] Consequently, there is a general demographic force over this period continually replenishing and increasing the population of labor force age, notwithstanding a reduced flow of newcomers over time.

This phenomenon should be more apparent in Exhibit 15, which presents the projected population between the ages of 15 to 64 years (again for the purposes of simplicity synonymizing this age span to that of the labor force years) for each of the benchmark years, as well as that which would have resulted if the 1970 base was aged as a closed system, i.e., assuming no migration. The gaps between the two are clearly evident. If New York City was a closed system, excluding both in- and outmigration, the population within the 15-to 64-years-of-age span would have increased by approximately 100,000 people over each five year interval. When migration is permitted to erode these recurrent gains (the projected population), the size of this age group is constrained to relatively fixed levels. Over each intervening period, the size of the group would continue to expand by the process of aging, only to be reduced at the end by migration losses.

Again, these data are but a simple illustration - defined in a format consistent with the preceding analyses - of the persistence with which New York City's labor force will expand over the next ten years. (The actual growth, of course, will be predicated on the evolution of the rate of participation of each age, sex, and color subpopulation). Economic stability in and of itself does not provide the capacity to absorb this expansion.

EXHIBIT 5-15

NEW YORK CITY POPULATION 15 TO 64 YEARS OF AGE, BASE PROJECTIONS VS. CLOSED SYSTEM AGING: 1970 TO 1985

Year	Projected Population (after migration)	Aged Base Population (absent migration)[1]
July 1, 1970 Base	5,071,708	5,071,708
1975	5,027,168	5,152,114
1980	5,117,745	5,249,998
1985	5,073,520	5,350,357

*Note:*1. The aged population was obtained by a closed system cohort survival analyses, assuming no migration. As of July 1 of the reported years.

Source: CUPR Projections.

Notes

1. For example, see: Subcommittee on the City of the Committee on Banking, Finance, and Urban Affairs, House of Representatives, How Cities Can Grow Old Gracefully (Washington, D.C.: U. S. Government Printing Office, 1977).

2. U. S. Bureau of the Census, Current Population Reports, Series P-20, No. 307, "Population Profile of the United States: 1976," U. S. Government Printing Office, Washington, D.C., 1977.

3. From 1920 to 1930, the population of New York City increased from 5.6 million to 6.9 million, a gain of 1.3 million people over ten years, or approximately 650,000 for each 5-year segment of the decade.

4. See George Sternlieb, Robert W. Burchell, and David Listokin, Rent Control in Miami Beach (New Brunswick: N.J.: Rutgers University, Center for Urban Policy Research, 1976) for a socioeconomic analysis of former New York City elderly residing in Miami.

5. In this context we are equating the baby boom to the births of the 1946 to 1957 period (see Chapter 4), although a longer time span is also appropriate for defining this cohort.

6. Obviously, the replacement process is of enormous complexity; it is certainly not a direct, one to one, substitution of newcomers for exiters. A chain of linked adjustments, akin to the housing filtering process, may be a more appropriate conceptualization for the broader process. However, in this analysis we are mainly concerned with the overall size dimension, not the internal dynamics.

Chapter 6

HOUSEHOLD IMPLICATIONS

INTRODUCTION

As forecasters we are all specialists in history. At best, we take a diffident little half-step into the future. But the direction of that half-step in very large part depends upon the segment of history from which we are extrapolating. If we view the events of the early post-1970 period as reflecting temporary cyclical adjustments, then our vision of the future will be quite different than that envisioned if these events are interpreted as a new foundation. The question persists whether short-run history is actually more enlightening than deceptive in terms of forecasting.

But, as has been stressed continuously in this study, there are secular forces whose momentum is unimpeded by the swings of other trendlines. The established parameters of the nation's age structure evolution - in particular the "battle of the bulge" - have been shown to dominate our population forecasts for New York City, even though migration demonstrates more volatile fluctuations. As we focus on households, we are confronted with an analogous situation - long-term national swings outweighing local immediacies.

Absolute population totals, even when examined via detailed age cohorts, at best sketch a partial picture of the city's demography. Of equal importance is the way individuals cluster into household configurations - groups of persons occupying individual housing units. Translated into households, the implications of population change for housing become much more apparent. Housing demand is not so much a function of total population size, but rather of the total number of households. Therefore, as we look to New York's immediate

EXHIBIT 6-1
HOUSEHOLD SIZE SHIFTS: 1950 TO 1976
(Persons per Household)

Year	Size
1950	3.37
1955	3.33
1960	3.33
1965	3.29
1970	3.14
1971	3.11
1972	3.06
1973	3.01
1974	2.97
1975	2.94
1976	2.89

Source: U.S. Bureau of the Census, Statistical Abstract of the United States: 1976. (97th Edition) Washington, D.C.,1976.

future, the patterns of gross demographic variation must
be viewed within the confines of household arrangements.
Again, the sheer force of the national trendline exerts
considerable influence upon the particulars of New York
City. Before presenting our household forecasts for
the city, then, the broader national context must be
reviewed.

THE NATIONAL CONTEXT

In the period of one generation covered by Exhibit
1, there has been a remarkably consistent decline in the
average household size in the United States. Between
1950 and 1976, the average number of persons per household has moved from 3.37 to 2.89, a decline of nearly
15 percent. The implications of this shift can be
emphasized by reference to a simple illustration.
Assume a political jurisdiction in 1950 has a base
population of 1,000 people; an average household size
of 3.37 persons results in 297 housing units. If by
1976 its absolute population size remains at the 1,000
person level, 346 housing units are implied by an average
household size of 2.89. Consequently, areas of overall
population stability or decline may still experience
growth in housing demand if the present household size
trends persist into the future.

A major contributor to changes in household size is
the number of children born to individual women. This
is reflected in Exhibit 2 which details the total children
born per 1,000 married women and the percent chilless
for women ever married for the years 1960, 1970, and 1976.
The import is very clear: for all the age groups up to
the age of 39 years, there is a substantial decrease
to the present time. (Those above 40 years of age in
1976 were the principle generators of the baby boom.)
Unless there is an unparalleled increase of women having
children in their later years, the future portends a continuation of the shrinking household size trendline.

As shown in the latter part of Exhibit 2, part of
the pattern of decline has been the result of the growing proportion of women under the age of 30 who are
married and have had not children. Again, this is a
phenomenon mainly of the women entering the childbearing
years in the wake of the baby boom.

Changing household size is not solely a function
of the rise and fall of the production of children; it
also results from changes in the basic marriage relationship. Shown in Exhibit 3 are two major barometers,

EXHIBIT 6-2
CHILDREN EVER BORN PER 1000 MARRIED WOMEN
AND PERCENT CHILDLESS FOR WOMEN EVER MARRIED:
1960 TO 1976[1]

Women Ever Married (Age)	Children Ever Born Per 1000 Women		
	1960	1970	1976
18 to 44 years	2,331	2,372	2,094
18 to 19 years	824	648	588
20 to 24 years	1,441	1,064	897
25 to 29 years	2,241	1,978	1,539
30 to 34 years	2,627	2,804	2,291
35 to 39 years	2,686	3,167	2,931
40 to 44 years	2,564	3,096	3,190
45 to 49 years	2,402	2,840	3,206

	Percent Childless for Women Ever Married		
	1960	1970	1976
15 to 44 years	15.0	16.4	18.8
15 to 19 years	43.6	50.7	55.1
20 to 24 years	24.2	35.9	41.7
25 to 29 years	12.6	15.8	21.7
30 to 34 years	10.4	9.3	10.5
35 to 39 years	11.1	7.4	6.6
40 to 44 years	14.1	8.6	7.5
45 to 49 years	18.1	10.8	7.8

Note:1. Data are for resident population in 1960 and 1970 and for
civilian noninstitutional population in 1976.

Source: U.S. Bureau of the Census, Current Population Reports,
Series P-20, No. 307, "Population Profile of the United
States: 1976," U.S. Government Printing Office,
Washington, D.C., April 1977.

EXHIBIT 6-3
MARRIAGE AND DIVORCE RATES: 1960-1976

Year	Marriage Rate [1]	Divorce Rate [2]
1950	11.1	2.6
1955	9.3	2.3
1960	8.5	2.2
1965	9.3	2.5
1970	10.6	3.5
1971	10.6	3.7
1972	11.0	4.1
1973	10.9	4.4
1974	10.5	4.6
1975	10.0	4.8
1976	9.9	5.0

Notes: 1. Number of marriages per 1000 population.
2. Number of divorces per 1000 population.

Source: U.S. National Center for Health Statistics, <u>Vital Statistics of the United States</u>, annual.

divorce and marriage rates. From 1960 to 1976, divorce
rates have increased by 127 percent, moving from 2.2
divorces per 1,000 population to the 5.0 level. The
marriage rate has exhibited less drastic swings, but
from 1972 to 1976 the number of marriages per 1,000
population has fallen from 11.0 to 9.9. Indeed, there
is some indication that the two indicators are converging.
In 1950, the divorce rate was 23.4 percent of the marriage rate; by 1976, this relationship increased to 50.5
percent. While not every divorce necessarily ends in
two separate households - with remarriage and other
alternative living arrangements possible - it is a significant force in generating additional households.

     Thus, broader changes in the American household are
apparent. The long-term decline in household size results
not only from declining fertility and fewer children but
also from an increasing divorce rate and a declining
marriage rate. Yet household size per se provides only
a surface glimpse at a very complex evolution. What are
the emerging household formats?

Emerging Household Formats

     Exhibit 4 details the composition of America's
households for 1960, 1970, and 1976. While the population growth from 1960 to 1970 was 13.6 percent, the
growth in households was 20.1 percent. In the 1970 to
1976 period, the former expanded by 5.2 percent while
the latter increased by 14.9 percent. Hence the gap
between the two rates of growth is widening substantially.

     The most salient household change is the decline in
importance of primary husband-wife families. In 1960,
they accounted for 74.3 percent of the nation's households. By 1976, their share had declined to 64.9 percent. At the same time, female-headed families (no
husband present) increased from 8.4 percent of the total
in 1960 to 10.1 percent in 1976. Overall, primary
families (related family members sharing a dwelling
unit), while not about to become extinct in America,
have declined from 85.0 percent of the total households
to 76.9 percent over this period of time.

     Households comprising primary individuals - persons
living alone or with nonrelatives only - increased quite
rapidly and presently (1976) account for 23.1 percent
of all households, as compared to 15.0 percent in 1960.
Indeed such nonfamily households increased more than
four times as fast as family households from 1970 to

EXHIBIT 6-4

HOUSEHOLDS BY TYPE AND SIZE: 1960 TO 1976[1]

(Numbers in thousands)

Subject	1960 Number	1960 Percent	1970 Number	1970 Percent	1976 Number	1976 Percent	Percent Change 1960-1970	Percent Change 1970-1976
Total Households	52,799	100.0	63,401	100.0	72,867	100.0	20.1	14.9
Primary Families	44,905	85.0	51,456	81.2	56,056	76.9	14.6	8.9
Husband-Wife	39,254	74.3	44,728	70.5	47,297	64.9	13.9	5.7
Male Head-No Wife Present	1,228	2.3	1,228	1.9	1,424	2.0	-	16.0
Female Head-No Husband Present	4,422	8.4	5,500	8.7	7,335	10.1	24.4	33.4
Primary Individuals	7,895	15.0	11,945	18.8	16,811	23.1	51.3	40.7
Living Alone[2]	6,896	13.1	10,851	17.1	14,983	20.6	57.4	38.1
With Nonrelative(s) Present	999	1.9	1,094	1.7	1,828	2.5	9.5	67.1
Average Size of Household	3.33		3.14		2.89			

Notes: 1. As of March of the respective years. Noninstitutional population excluding Armed Forces in barracks.
2. One person households.

Source: U.S. Bureau of the Census, Current Population Reports, Series P-20, No. 307, "Population Profile of the United States: 1976," U.S. Government Printing Office, Washington, D.C. April 1977.

EXHIBIT 6-5

TWO PERSON PRIMARY INDIVIDUAL HOUSEHOLDS BY AGE: 1970 TO 1975[1]

(Numbers in thousands)[2]

Age of Household Head (Primary Individual)	1970			1976		
	Primary Individuals in 2 Person House-holds	*Sharing With Un-related Persons of Opposite Sex*		*Primary Individuals in 2 Person House-holds*	*Sharing With Un-related Persons of Opposite Sex*	
		Number	*Percent*		*Number*	*Percent*
Total	991	327	33.0	1,479	660	44.6
Under 25 years	270	29	10.7	497	155	31.2
25 to 44 years	257	60	23.3	580	270	46.6
45 to 64 years	231	123	53.2	250	153	61.2
65 years and over	234	115	49.1	152	83	54.6

Notes: 1. Noninstitutional population excluding Armed Forces in barracks.
2. Numbers may not add due to rounding.

Source: U.S. Bureau of the Census, Current Population Reports, Series P-20, No. 307, "Population Profile of the United States: 1976," U.S. Government Printing Office, Washington, D.C., April 1977.

1976 (40.7 percent versus 8.9 percent). This is the result of a substantial increase in single-person households, which had doubled in number to about the 15 million level by 1976, as well as of the emergence of a relatively new phenomenon, households comprising primary individuals and nonrelatives. In the six years from 1970 to 1976, this household type had the fastest growth rate of those shown here, increasing by 67.1 percent.

If we focus on the percentage changes for the latter period, the sharpness of the current trendlines - partially obscured by the longer time span - becomes evident. The number of households headed by primary individuals from 1970 to 1976 increased by 40.7 percent while primary families with female heads (no husband present) increased by 33.4 percent. Even male-headed primary families with no wife present increased by 16.0 percent. At the same time, however, the classic husband and wife families expanded by only 5.7 percent. Consequently, what were once unique or atypical households are dominating the recent growth increment and require further analysis.

Two Person Households

A significant portion of the primary individual households with nonrelatives present comprise two person households (1.5 million out of 1.8 million such households in 1976). Exhibit 5 details their configuration by age of the household head for 1970 and 1976. The most significant increase occurred in the number of primary individuals who share their living quarters with an unrelated person of the opposite sex. Indeed, their number more than doubled, increasing from 327,000 in 1970 to 660,000 in 1976, and their percentage share of the total number of two person households increased from 33.0 percent to 44.6 percent. While this phenomenon was mainly the province of older households in 1970, the critical mass, in terms of absolute numbers, has shifted to the younger age cohorts. But this is not merely a new fashion for America's young adults. The 25 to 44 years of age category accounts for 40.9 percent (270,000) of the households of this genre, the largest single concentration.

While the rate of increase has been remarkable for the latter living arrangement, it should be emphasized that they account for only 3.9 percent of all primary individual households (660,000 out of 16.8 million), and are outnumbered by single-person households by almost 23 to one (15.0 million to 660,000).

While other household types are also gaining promi-
inence, this abbreviated review should indicate both
the reality and the import of the national trendlines.
And, as was the case with population in the aggregate,
New York City is not immune to the forces impacting
the nation as a whole. Despite the lack of detailed
intercensal elaborations of New York's households comparable to the national equivalent, we can be assured
that the city will reflect the national pattern. Consequently, the preceding trendlines provide a reference
framework - an evaluative logic - for undertaking and
interpreting the city forecasts.

THE NATIONAL-NEW YORK CITY PATTERN: 1960 TO 1970

The relationship between the changes in population
and households for both New York City and the nation are
depicted in Exhibit 6. Over the 1960 to 1970 intercensal period, the number of households nationally increased by 19.7 percent, while the total population expanded by only 13.3 percent. Consequently, households
were increasing at a rate of 1.48 times that of the
overall population.

New York City experienced even greater disparities
between population growth and the formation of new
households over the 1960 to 1970 period. While the population growth is gauged by a rate of increase of only
1.5 percent, the number of households were ·expanding
by 6.9 percent. Households, then, were increasing at a
rate 4.6 times that attendant to population growth.
Indeed, 1.6. households were secured for every person
added to the city's population base (181,970   113,579).

Another indicator relevance to both observational
areas is household size. While both New York City and
the nation experienced considerable shrinkage in household size over the 1960 to 1970 period - slightly below
and above 5 percent, respectively - the city's households
were consistently smaller than their national counterparts. In 1960, the average size of the national household was 1.156 times greater (3.33÷2.88) than that of
New York; by 1970, it was 1.146 times greater. This
barely perceptible narrowing hints that the limits of
family fragmentation have yet to be reached in New York;
it also provides some indication that in the future the
rate of household formation in New York City will tend
to lag that of the nation, although not by an appreciable
magnitude.

EXHIBIT 6-6
NEW YORK CITY AND THE NATION:
1960 TO 1970

A. Household and Population Change

	1960	1970	Change: 1960 to 1970 Number	Percent
United States				
Households	53,023,875	63,449,747	10,425,872	19.7
Population	179,323,175	203,235,298	23,912,123	13.3

$$\frac{\text{Household Growth Rate}}{\text{Population Growth Rate}} = \frac{19.7}{13.3} = 1.48$$

	1960	1970	Change: 1960 to 1970 Number	Percent
New York City				
Households	2,654,902	2,836,872	181,970	6.9
Population	7,781,984	7,894,862	113,579	1.5

$$\frac{\text{Household Growth Rate}}{\text{Population Growth Rate}} = \frac{6.9}{1.5} = 4.60$$

- -

B. Household Size Changes

	1960	1970	Change: 1960 to 1970 Number	Percent
United States	3.33	3.14	-.19	-5.7
New York City	2.88	2.74	-.14	-4.9

Note: Data is for April 1 of the respective years.

Source: U.S. Bureau of the Census.

THE PROJECTIONS

The household projection methodology has been more
fully detailed in Chapter 1. Suffice it to reiterate
that the major procedure has been to apply the projected
national parameters - scaled or calibrated to historic
(1960 to 1970) nation-local differentials - to the projected population bases of New York City. Hence the
assumption is that the city will parallel the projected
national experience, but it will continue to reflect
past differences.

Between 1970 and 1985, the following changes in
New York City's households and population are projected:

Year	Population	Households
1970 (April 1)	7,894,862	2,836,872
1975 (July 1)	7,490,690	2,857,176
1980 (July 1)	7,391,510	2,981,649
1985 (July 1)	7,231,198	3,086,315

The number of households continues to increase
even in the context of overall population contraction.
It should be pointed out, however, that the national
Series A projections were employed as a base, the highest
series of household projections (see Exhibit 8). If
more conservative national parameters had been used, the
projected number of households in New York City would
obviously be smaller than that presented above, yet
positive gains in the number of households would still
be registered over the 1975 to 1985 period. Despite
continued contraction in the city's overall population
size, the demand for housing, as gauged by the number
of projected households, should increase.

A further elaboration of the projections is presented in Exhibit 7, which partitions the number of
households by the age of the household head. As in the
case of total population, the baby boom generation exerts
the most powerful influence. Indeed, vigorous growth
in the number of households whose head is between 25
and 44 years of age over the 1975 to 1985 period far
outweighs the decline in the number of more mature
households. From a base of 1.1 million in 1975, those
households headed by an individual between 25 and 44
years of age should increase to almost 1.6 million by
1985, an increase of about .5 million households. And,
to the degree that population declines could be arrested,
the resulting household totals would have even more
significant implications for the city's residential
markets.

EXHIBIT 6-7
NUMBER OF HOUSEHOLDS BY AGE OF THE HEAD OF THE
HOUSEHOLD, NEW YORK CITY: 1970, 1975, 1980, 1985

Age	1970	1975	1980	1985
Under 24	168,407	199,268	214,808	200,740
25-34	526,474	691,942	836,626	896,801
35-44	494,130	420,266	485,497	658,535
45-64	1,050,804	932,485	821,710	714,496
65+	597,057	613,215	623,008	615,743
TOTAL	1,826,872	1,857,176	1,981,649	3,086,315

Note: As of July 1 of the respective years, except for 1970, which is April 1.

Source: CUPR Projections.

EXHIBIT 6-8
NUMBER OF HOUSEHOLDS BY AGE OF THE HEAD OF HOUSEHOLD, UNITED STATES: 1970, 1975, 1980, 1985[1]
(Numbers in thousands)

Age	1970	1975	1980	1985
Under 24	4,634	6,143	7,088	7,387
25-34	11,643	15,189	18,487	21,174
35-44	11,776	11,746	13,482	16,797
45-64	23,158	24,331	24,794	25,149
65+	12,239	14,360	16,102	17,949
TOTAL	63,450	71,769	79,953	88,456

Notes: 1. These are the Series A projections, which define the highest rates of household formation.

Source: U.S. Bureau of the Census, Current Population Reports, Series P-25, No. 607, "Projections of the Number of Households and Families: 1975 to 1990," U.S. Government Printing Office, Washington, D.C. 1975.

The patterns isolated in Exhibit 7 are the result of two major developments. First, they are a derivative of the evolving population age structure of New York City - the household age profile directly reflects the population developments detailed in the preceding chapter. Second, they are a consequence of changing headship rates, which operationalize the broader transformation toward smaller household configurations. The confluence of the aging baby boom progeny and the increasing headship rates across the age spectrum results in a marked surge in the number of households in the 25-to 44-years-of-age categories. And, the changes registered in the remaining household age sectors - where in general the population equivalents are contracting - are mitigated by the increasing rates of headship.

As a frame of reference for these anticipations, the national projections are presented in Exhibit 8. In the aggregate, the similarities and disparities between the national and local patterns mirror those exhibited in the population analyses. In both cases, the age sectors (25 to 44 years of age) encompassing the baby boom generation dominate the growth ledgers. In contrast, those age sectors in which New York City's population change varied from that of the nation - the shrinkage characterizing those over 45 years of age - persist as they are reflected in households. Nonetheless, it is apparent that the city, for the most part, represents a minor variation of the national phenomenon.

Household Types

Another important dimension of this analysis is the mix of household formats. In Exhibit 9, the national projections are detailed according to the partitions used in Exhibit 4. It should be noted that the projections were made in 1975 based upon Current Population Survey data through 1975. Significantly, the 1976 estimates (see Exhibit 4) approach the pattern projected for 1980, a much faster rate than had been anticipated, suggesting that the projections understate the evolving profile of household types. Nonetheless, primary individual households represent the major growth sector while primary husband and wife families decline in relative importance (see Exhibit 9).

The pattern of change projected for New York City closely corresponds with that of the nation (see Exhibit 10), with the city at the cutting edge of the national transformation. Indeed, the proportion of husband and wife families is expected to fall below 50

EXHIBIT 6-9
PROJECTIONS OF THE MIX OF HOUSEHOLD TYPES, UNITED STATES: 1970 TO 1985

Household Type	March 1, 1970	March 1, 1976	July 1, 1980	July 1, 1985
Total Households	100.0	100.0	100.0	100.0
Primary Families	81.2	76.9	76.6	75.0
Husband-Wife	70.5	64.9	64.8	63.0
Other Male Head	1.9	2.0	2.0	1.9
Other Female Head	8.7	10.1	9.8	10.1
Primary Individuals	18.8	23.1	23.4	25.0

Sourcec: U.S. Bureau of the Census, Current Population Reports, Series P-20, No. 311, "Household and Family Characteristics: March 1976," U.S. Government Printing Office, Washington, D.C. 1977; U.S. Bureau of the Census, Current Population Reports, Series P-25, No. 607, "Projections of the Number of Households and Families: 1975 to 1990," U.S. Government Printing Office, Washington, D.C. 1975.

EXHIBIT 6-10
PROJECTIONS OF THE MIX OF HOUSEHOLD TYPES
NEW YORK CITY: 1970 TO 1985

Household Type	April 1, 1970	July 1, 1975	July 1, 1980	July 1, 1985
Total Households	100.0	100.0	100.0	100.0
Primary Families	72.1	69.6	67.6	65.9
Husband-Wife	56.5	53.2	51.3	49.3
Other Male Head	3.1	2.8	2.6	2.6
Other Female Head	12.5	13.6	13.7	14.0
Primary Individuals	27.9	30.4	32.4	34.1

Source: CUPR Projections.

percent by 1985, while primary individual households increase their share to 34.1 percent. New York City may see the fabled "modular" American household fall into distinct minority status.

These shifts are expressed in absolute numbers in Exhibit 11. The bulk of the household additions between 1970 and 1985 will comprise primary individuals (single-person households or two or more unrelated individuals sharing a housing unit) - a growth of approximately 260,000 households - and female-headed families, with an additional 77,000 households secured by the latter category. The remaining formats show very little change.

This pattern of household formats is the logical accompaniment to diminishing household sizes. In both New York City and the nation, the trendlines evidenced over the previous decade are expected to persist in the future, although at a slightly reduced pace (see Exhibit 12). While New York City continues to exhibit household sizes smaller than the national counterparts, the gap between the two narrows by 1985.

SUMMARY

The evolution of the nation's household configurations maintains the pace of change evidenced by its economic and population parameters. While the latter have tended to evolve to the general disadvantage of New York City, the household transformation appears to be a more positive development. The trend to smaller sizes and configurations serves to bolster the demand for housing at a time when absolute population declines may be inexorable.

1. Over the last intercensal period (1960 to 1970), the average household size in the United States has declined from 3.33 to 3.14 persons. In contrast, New York City's average size of household has shifted from 2.88 to 2.74 persons during the corresponding period.

2. These changes document a long-term national trend toward smaller housholds. New York City is at the leading edge of this transformation.

3. Smaller housholds and rapid rates of household formation imply a demand for housing far in excess of that indicated by population growth alone. From 1970 to 1976, the number of house-

EXHIBIT 6-11
NEW YORK CITY HOUSEHOLD FORMATS
1970 TO 1985

Household Type	April 1, 1970	July 1, 1975	July 1, 1980	July 1, 1985
Total Households	2,836,872	2,857,176	2,981,649	3,086,315
Primary Families	2,043,765	1,987,650	2,015,893	2,032,030
Husband-Wife	1,603,387	1,520,741	1,527,797	1,520,936
Other Male Head	86,686	78,580	78,417	79,936
Other Female Head	353,692	388,329	409,679	431,158
Primary Individuals	793,107	869,526	965,756	1,054,285

Source: CUPR Projections.

EXHIBIT 6-12
HOUSEHOLD SIZE CHANGES, NEW YORK CITY
AND THE UNITED STATES: 1960 TO 1985

Year	New York City	United States
1960	2.88	3.33
1970	2.74	3.14
1975	2.59	2.92
1980	2.45	2.73
1985	2.32	2.60

Source: U.S. Bureau of the Census, <u>Current Population Reports</u>, Series P-25, No. 607, "Projections of the Number of Households and Families: 1975 to 1990," U.S. Government Printing Office, Washington, D.C., 1975; CUPR Projections.

holds in the nation increased from 63.4 million
to 72.9 million, a growth rate of 14.9 percent.
At the same time, the nation's population increased by 5.2 percent. The differential between
these growth rates has widened over time.

4. By 1976, the average national household size had
   declined to 2.89 persons. The reduced level of
   fertility, soaring divorce rates, and declining
   marriage rates are all significant in this regard. As a result, traditional husband-wife
   families are the nation's slowest growing household type. The fastest growing are primary individual households, either single persons living
   alone or with nonrelatives present. Again, as
   reflected by household size, New York City's
   skew toward more "nontraditional" families is
   more accentuated than that of the nation.

5. The national projections portend a virtual surge
   in household formations. Between 1975 and 1985,
   the number of households in the United States
   is projected to increase from 71.8 million to
   88.5 million, a gain of almost one-quarter
   (23.5 percent) over a ten-year span.

6. As a result of the events and forces in motion,
   the number of households in New York City also
   will show considerable growth through 1985,
   despite the projection of continued population
   decline. Between 1975 and 1985, the city's
   resident households will increase from 2.86
   million to 3.09 million - the city will secure
   almost 230,000 additional households at the
   same time that its population losses approach
   260,000 people.

7. Virtually all of the household gains of New
   York City, and the bulk of those of the nation,
   are the province of the 25⁻to 44⁻years⁻of⁻age
   sectors, into which the baby boom fully matures
   by 1985.

8. The emerging formats will be dominated by primary individual households, composed of either
   a single individual or two or more unrelated
   individuals, while the traditional husband-
   wife family will decline in both relative and
   absolute terms. Both New York City and the
   nation will be characterized by the ascension
   of atypical household types.

9. Gauging this transformation is the continued contraction in the average size of both the nation's
   and the city's households. The city's households still will reflect historic differentials -
   a skew toward smaller sizes - but the gap between the two narrows through the projection interval.